Contemporary Cases in Labor–Management Relations

Lynn P. Cooke

R&I Associates

William N. Cooke

Graduate School of Business Administration
and Joint Center for Labor-Management Relations
University of Michigan

1989

**BPI
IRWIN**

Homewood, Illinois 60430

Cover photo: Robert Frerck, TSW-CLICK/Chicago

Executive editor: Gary L. Nelson
Project editor: Suzanne Ivester
Production manager: Carma W. Fazio
Cover design: Jeanne Wolfgeher
Compositor: Carlisle Communications, Ltd.
Typeface: 10/12 Palatino
Printer: Arcata Graphics/Kingsport

LIBRARY OF CONGRESS
Library of Congress Cataloging-in-Publication Data

Cooke, Lynn P.
    Contemporary cases in labor-management relations / Lynn P. Cooke,
William N. Cooke.
        p. cm.
    ISBN 0-256-06654-X (pbk.)
    1. Industrial relations—Case studies.   2. Collective bargaining-
Case studies.   3. Case method.   I. Cooke, William N.   II. Title.
HD6971.C77 1989
331—dc19   88–14879
                                                                            CIP

Printed in the United States of America
1 2 3 4 5 6 7 8 9 0   K   5 4 3 2 1 0 9 8

Dedicated to Bill's grandmother Sally and Lynn's brother Gil—neither of whom was impressed nor surprised by this endeavor.

Preface

Except for the occasional mock negotiation, grievance, and arbitration exercise, most educators in labor-management relations rely exclusively on the classic lecture-discussion method of classroom instruction. The authors initially shared a widely held belief that the so-called case method lacks rigor and, especially, generalizability. With exposure to the strengths of the case method, however, our strong skepticism (if not benign disdain) changed.

As a professor of labor-management relations, the second author read far too many course evaluations questioning the applicability of labor-management theory, taught within the lecture-discussion format, to the real world. As a result, he began experimenting with case exercises several years ago. Since much of the subject matter of labor-management relations involves disputes and problem resolution (sometimes in win-lose and sometimes in potential, but not obvious, win-win settings), he discovered that assigned student advocacy roles generated lively and heated case discussion. He also discovered that another benefit of the case method arose from putting future managers, union leaders, and policy makers in the other party's shoes, encouraging students to shed (at least for the moment) previous stereotypes about the other side. In short, when properly handled, the case method proved an ideal complement to traditional classroom instruction in labor-management relations.

The first author, in pursuing her MBA, encountered some 400 cases in two years of coursework. Accompanying broader theory, she found that well-written and orchestrated cases provided an optimal learning experience across disciplines. Moreover, there were many cases available on most business topics. Unfortunately, labor-management relations instructors seeking to integrate cases into their coursework either have had to develop their own cases—a very time-consuming proposition— or rely on the sparse supply of published cases, most of which are outdated and/or limited in their focus or scope. Hence, the primary objective of this book is to begin filling that void, providing a set of cases rich in contemporary and vital labor-management issues.

All of the cases are set in the 1980s. Each case includes background on the business or employing organization, the union, the labor-management history, and the evolution of the problem or problems to be resolved. All except two of the cases are based on actual company-union relations. Much time was spent gathering field information to enrich publicly available data, or at times to discard it. The authors spoke with union leaders (both local and national), managers and executives, counsel, the National Labor Relations Board (both the regional offices and the General Counsel), community spokespersons, and lobbyists.

Each case takes students to a certain point and requires them to negotiate a resolution or make recommendations and provides instructors with rich background information on current applications of some traditional labor-management concepts. These include the concept of due process and random drug testing; the duty to bargain in good faith issues of successorship, Chapter 11 proceedings, subcontracting, and transference of work offshore or to domestic nonunion facilities; and changes in the relative economic power of management and the unions in the face of changing environmental factors. Each case explains how the problems or issues were resolved at the time and provides an update of what happened since resolution.

Most of the cases have stood the test of regular classroom use; several have also been used successfully in executive training programs. Students readily adopt their advocacy roles, and classroom discussion quickly becomes spirited. One group of manufacturing executives, in the role of the union, even printed union stickers shortly after the start of a case exercise.

THE PLAN OF THE BOOK

The first three sections of the book are patterned after the unionization process: organizing, negotiations, and contract administration. The text begins with cases concerning illegal campaign conduct and then moves to three long cases covering contemporary negotiations issues. Two of these cases include such issues as subcontracting, concession bargaining, and employee involvement programs; the third case, on Louisiana-Pacific, covers contemporary problems of traditional strike activity during contract negotiations. The third section of the book examines contract administration, including cases on grievance handling (one within the public sector) and the duty of fair representation. The final section of the book is devoted to cases covering transitions within labor-management relations that have become prevalent over the last decade. Here students may observe that not only the issues but the process of labor-management relations is under review.

ACKNOWLEDGMENT

In writing this text the authors worked together to select key contemporary issues and problems that would be most relevant to students' future careers, to frame the overall objectives of the set of cases, and to identify cases that fit these objectives. Lynn then assimilated the information, laid out detailed frameworks, and wrote the cases. Bill provided final editorial comments, generally in the form of squiggles and question marks.

Thus, although it is highly irregular to do so, the authors wish to thank each other for the support they've shown one another during the writing of this text. Many authors dedicate completed volumes to their spouses as an apology for long hours away from home and preoccupation when at home. In our case, the work simply became part of our homelife, providing intriguing issues for eleventh-hour discussions and debates.

Lynn P. Cooke
William N. Cooke

A Note to Students

You will leave your training grounds and enter the real world armed with facts, figures, and definitions. Alone, these are of little value in the dynamic, real-world environment. You must also distinguish between important versus peripheral facts; determine the importance of implicit as well as explicit information; and understand that there is often no "right" answer, but merely an optimal alternative under the present circumstances. These are decision-making skills. The case teaching method exercises and develops your decision-making ability.

CASE METHOD AND LABOR RELATIONS

1. Decision Making. Many business functions determine optimal outcomes based on single objectives, such as market share, internal rate of return, or capacity utilization. In labor-management relations, however, decisions evolve from and directly impact three separate groups: the company, the union, and the workforce. Indirectly, decisions affect the community and other stakeholders. All of these groups put forth their own arguments, needs, and positions. Thus, the information level increases proportionately. Within the simulated environment of the case, you need to:

1. Sort, prioritize, and apply information to generate alternatives.
2. Project alternative outcomes.

2. Role-Playing. Armed with identical information, labor and management personnel often arrive at disparate conclusions. In case analysis, you will gain practice reviewing all sides of an issue. Paralleling in vitro labor-management relations, you will be appointed either a management or a union advocate. This role-playing will increase your understanding of your opponents' interests, needs, problems, concerns, and, hence, viewpoints. In turn, it will prepare you to be a better advocate.

3. Communicating. Good communication skills are vital in any successful career. Labor-management relations in particular requires interpersonal and negotiation skills, especially since it is full of the nuances of legal phrasing. Case discussion encourages two key aspects of these skills: the ability to listen and the ability to articulate.

AN ANALYTICAL FRAMEWORK

Optimizing solutions in any instant case demands a comprehensive analytical framework applicable to future work-related challenges. The labor-management relations world continually changes. New technology, rising global and domestic nonunion competition, declining manufacturing unionization, increasing service unionization, public policy and the law, and labor-management collaboration and employee involvement are just a few new factors. Many such factors rapidly emerged during the past 10 years; ten years hence, the "new" factors may again be quite different.

While the specific cases in this volume were selected for the timeliness of the subject matter, the goal of the text is to increase your decision-making ability in all foreseen and unforeseen situations. By consistently applying a general framework for analyzing cases, you will find optimal, informed solutions more readily than by reviewing cases in a haphazard fashion.

A fairly generic framework that has guided the selection and development of the cases follows. No attempt is made here, however, to identify or detail all the factors that might apply to any given case. Instead, the framework points out that the parties must examine and weigh a great range of factors, from the broader economic and socio-political environments, to the specific organizational environment or context unique to any labor-management relationship. Other assigned readings and instruction will build upon the suggested framework. Moreover, like practitioners, you will allow your own knowledge, experience, and intuition to fill in and color the analytical framework you explicitly or implicitly use. Stretching your thinking beyond the classroom walls will better prepare you for what lies ahead.

A General Framework

I. Economic environment.
 A. Product (service) market competition.
  1. Nature of market (growth or mature).
  2. Number and type of global and domestic competitors.
  3. Extent of unionization.
 B. Labor market conditions.
  1. Supply and demand for skilled, semi-skilled, and unskilled labor.

2. Labor market demographics.
3. Workforce values.

II. Sociopolitical environment.
   A. Public ideologies and values toward labor and management.
   B. Labor laws and regulations.
      1. NLRA, LMRA, and NLRB policies and procedures.
      2. State public sector laws.
      3. Right-to-work legislation.
   C. Public policies.
      1. International trade regulations.
      2. Antitrust regulation and industry deregulation.
      3. Social policies (affirmative action, occupational health and safety, environmental).

III. Organizational environments.
   A. Company structure and strategies.
      1. Size, number of facilities, product lines.
      2. Financial, production, and marketing strategies.
      3. Plants and locations (domestic, offshore).
      4. Management styles (authoritarian, participative).
   B. Union structure and politics.
      1. Size and number of locals.
      2. Local, regional, national authority.
      3. Industry penetration.
      4. Homogeneity of membership and leadership.
   C. Collective bargaining structure and relationship.
      1. Single company; master and/or local agreements; one or more unions.
      2. Multiemployer; single or multiunion agreements.
      3. Percent of company unionization.
      4. Hostile or cooperative relations.
   D. Technical context.
      1. Mode of operation (batch, continuous, job shop).
      2. Capital intensity.
      3. Level of technology (high, low, or service).
      4. Skill and technical level of workforce.
   E. Key personalities (management and union).

CASE PREPARATION

Because case learning is student activated, a case will only "play" if you attend class extremely well prepared. Case preparation is a unique learning process. While every student eventually discovers an optimal personal learning process, case preparation requires five basic steps:

1. Understanding the situation.
2. Framing the problem.

3. Determining the objectives.
4. Generating alternatives and outcomes.
5. Choosing an alternative.

Each of these will be discussed briefly. While step 1 necessarily requires individual preparation, small group interaction prior to classroom discussion increases learning inherent in the remaining steps.

Step 1. Understanding the Situation.   In order to fully understand the situation presented within a case, you must be familiar with the case. This is accomplished by taking the time to read it more than once. Ideally, the first reading should occur as soon as the assignment is known. Avoid attempting analysis at this point; this first reading is for getting the feel of the situation. The human mind remains quite active in neutral, so allow the information to incubate in the back of your mind before re-reading the case and starting analysis in earnest.

During and after the second reading, take notes. This is the information-gathering process. Trends, anomolies, discrepancies, and facts for the framework should all be jotted down. Next, analyze.

Step 2. Framing the Problem.   Every case provides an abundance of information. As in the real world, some of it is useful, some of it is not. In this step, refine the information, determining one or two key issues. Many students new to the case method encounter difficulty with this step. There may be many minor problems; are these informational "noise," or do they add to the major problem? Is a seemingly minor problem at the root of a larger problem? Does any real problem exist? With practice, you will become more adept at focusing your analysis.

Step 3. Determining Objectives for the Root of the Problem.   Having defined the key problem, what are the objectives of the parties? Are they in concert with one another? Often the goals of middle management may differ from those of upper management, and the goals of the union membership may differ from those of the union leadership. As a result, disparate objectives may become part of the problem. Understanding these disparate objectives, however, forces you to generate a wider variety of alternatives in an effort to discover common interests rather than focusing upon conflicting positions.

Define objectives clearly and specifically. If there is more than one key problem, list specific objectives separately. If the objective seems too narrow, such as "get a $3 per hour wage concession," rethink *why* such a concession is necessary in the broader context. Is it that the ratio of labor costs to total costs is too high? Or is it that production costs in general are too high? Thinking about this issue encourages you to generate alternatives addressing the root of the problem, rather than just its symptoms.

Step 4. Generating Alternatives and Outcomes. Having defined the problem and stated the objectives, brainstorm through a series of alternatives without critiquing them. In many instances, the case implies alternatives available to the parties. However, do not be constrained by these options; one of your original alternatives may indeed prove even better. Then, project the direct and indirect consequences of each alternative. For example, if you were to gain a $3 per hour concession from the workers, would the labor climate become so adversarial that absenteeism would increase and overall productivity decrease? If this were the case, then your alternative would not, as a whole, decrease production costs.

Step 5. Choosing an Alternative. Having generated alternatives and outcomes, the final step is to choose an action and defend it as compared with the rejected alternatives. It is critical that you take this final step. It is the most important step in case analysis—the decision. Having read hundreds of case analyses, the authors discovered that many students copiously list alternatives only to forego taking action.

Although there is no research on case-analysis psychosis, the authors speculate that this fear of action is a fear of being graded right or wrong. There is no right or wrong in the final alternative; failure results only from haphazard analysis, or insufficient alternative-generation. The Ford Edsel, for example, was not a failure per se. Ford's decision to build the American dream car was a sound one. The company failed only by relying on an internal opinion of what Americans wanted, instead of extensive market research. This is an example of haphazard analysis. Decision making which stems from thorough analysis, extensive alternative generation, and sound defense is theoretically optimal.

CLASS DISCUSSION: A.L.B.

The greatest test for analytical thoroughness is a meeting of the minds. In order to take full advantage of the amazing variety of thought from your colleagues, you must learn the art of fruitful case discussion: Articulate, Listen, Build.

Articulate. Much like reporters in a press conference, your colleagues are looking for that 10-second segment they can air to the world. The other 29 minutes and 50 seconds are lost forever. Organize your thoughts and state your position as succinctly as possible. Make a point, or raise a key issue; but remember, your classmates' attention spans are no longer than yours.

Listen.   Succinct expression increases the likelihood that classmates will listen actively to one another. To listen effectively, always look at the speaker. Take short notes to jog your own thinking. Ask for clarification if necessary. Remain attentive to the discussion—there is nothing more annoying than someone reiterating what has already been covered.

Build.   Participants must build progressively upon the discussion; each comment should add value to the previous one, or challenge it, serving to refine and augment individuals' ideas. Many case instructors let the class carry on the discussion without interruption, intervening only at the end to summarize key points; others direct students' thinking, raising issues and challenging positions.

SUMMARY

The case teaching method provides an opportunity for active learning within a simulated work environment. In addition to learning basic elements of labor-management relations, students develop decision-making skills and gain valuable experience in both labor and management advocacy.

Three basic experiences of the case method readily transcend classroom walls. First, the analytical experience broadens students' active knowledge base, making them accustomed to confronting mountains of information. Second, the interactive classroom experience increases communication skills. And third, the adversarial element of case discussion prepares students for the interpersonal dynamics of their careers, including confrontation both across the table and within an organization.

CONTENTS

Contemporary Cases in Labor–Management Relations

Union Organizing

General Hospital and the Service Employees' International Union

The Service Employees' International Union (SEIU) Local 275, AFL-CIO, alleged numerous independent 8(a)(1) and 8(a)(3) violations by Baton Rouge General Hospital between January 27, 1981 and April 10, 1981, during a union organizing campaign. On April 10, 1981 the regional director of Region 15 of the National Labor Relations Board (NLRB) consolidated three of the unfair labor practice complaints. Alleged questionable campaign conduct included:

8(a)(1) Violations

1. That management illegally announced improved benefits during an election campaign.
2. That management, its officers, agents, and representatives threatened employees with job loss if they voted for SEIU Local 275.
3. That employees were threatened with loss of previously enjoyed benefits for engaging in protected, concerted, and/or union activities.
4. That agents of management continued to coerce workers against the union from about February 9, 1981 through May 7, 1981, the date of the NLRB certification election.

8(a)(3) Violations

That management discriminatorily:

1. Laid off eight employees
2. Changed the work assignment of one employee
3. Terminated one employee

for their participation in union organizing activities.

---

*This case was based upon a March 1987 National Labor Relations Board decision.

EVENTS LEADING TO ALLEGED 8(A)(1) VIOLATIONS

On November 24, 1980, the SEIU Local 275 notified Baton Rouge General Hospital that a union organizing campaign was ongoing at the hospital and supplied the hospital with a list of employees on the organizing committee.

Improved Benefits

On November 28, the hospital comptroller informed Claude Kilpatrick, hospital president, that changes in Medicare allowed an annual hospital reimbursement of $54,000 for staff parking. Currently, the hospital charged employees $4.62 per pay period, totaling $50,000 per year. In a notice dated December 2, 1980, the hospital advised all employees that effective December 14, employees would no longer be charged for parking in the hospital garage.

In a memo dated January 12, 1981, the hospital notified employees that "effective January 1, 1981, the board of trustees has approved a retirement program which is fully funded by the hospital." Until this announcement, the hospital utilized the Southern Baptist Annuity Board (SBAB), which required an employee pension contribution. However, hospital board meeting minutes indicated that the SBAB's low interest rate and complications due to ERISA amendments were topics of board discussion from May 4, 1979 through December 22, 1980. A private insurance company, Union Mutual, had submitted a pension plan proposal to the hospital on July 10, 1980. Employee Retirement Income Security Act (ERISA) amendments effective September 1980 disallowed the hospital's continued church exemptions as a former church institution in the SBAB. On December 22, 1980 the personnel committee of the board of trustees was notified that retirement funds would be placed with Union Mutual effective January 1, 1981.

Coercion

Employee Mary Ann Hickman went into supervisor Era McRae's office on October 20, 1980 to request a change in her work schedule so that she could attend a friend's funeral. Hickman claims that after granting her request, McRae initiated the following conversation:

McRae:

I know you've heard about what's going on with the union.

Hickman:

No. I've been out sick for over a month, so I don't know too much about anything going on.

McRae:

> Well, let me tell you about it. If we had a union here, we wouldn't be able to talk like we are doing now. You wouldn't be able to talk about schedules. And you might be bargaining with your benefits. When they sit down to bargain they don't mean that the hospital has to agree with what they ask for. And you could lose your benefits.

According to McRae, the director of nursing instructed her to inform employees how the hospital felt about the union. However, McRae admitted that as supervisor of 175 employees, she didn't know whether or not she had had a conversation with Hickman—and that, in fact, she wouldn't recognize Hickman if she saw her.

On December 7, several union activists, including Susan Quiett and Teresa Thomas, distributed union handbills during their break. Claude Kilpatrick, hospital president, approached Thomas and asked to see some of her "propaganda." Kilpatrick read the leaflet, then stated, "It will never work." Thomas replied, "Well, there's nothing wrong with trying." Kilpatrick laughed, then walked on.

Housekeeping supervisor Eva Lewis saw the handbilling while leaving the hospital. She approached Quiett and asked her if she knew what she was doing. Quiett replied that she did. Lewis then reentered the hospital to report the activity to another supervisor.

On December 8, Quiett was reassigned to three different work areas during her shift—her first such reassignment since being employed by the hospital. Shortly thereafter, Quiett was assigned to clean and mop walls and floors in pediatrics and then to sweep and mop five flights of stairs. Such jobs were typically assigned to porters. Additionally, Quiett was assigned to clean 42 rooms without help. Her request for assistance was denied by her supervisor.

On December 10, employee Bertha Smith claimed she was approached by Robert Mancell, chief X-ray technician, in one of the X-ray rooms. According to Smith, Mancell asked her if she had heard whether they were trying to organize a union at the hospital and how she felt about the union. Smith told Mancell that a union wouldn't be such a bad idea. Mancell retorted that his son participated in a union, and that if the union went on strike, Smith might not get her job back.

Mancell denied the one-on-one conversation, but indicated he had a meeting with several employees in which he "just wanted to hear what they had to say . . . just [to see] if they had an opinion." In addition to the meeting, Mancell admitted that he approached two other employees with the same question.

On January 15, 1981, the union filed its representation petition in accordance with NLRB procedures. Around the same time, Gerald Colston, manager of general stores, approached employee Yolanda Scott. According to Scott, the following conversation ensued:

Colston:

Do you know anything about the union?

Scott:

Yea.

Colston:

Been to any meetings?

Scott:

No. My grandmother's been real sick in the hospital, so I haven't partici-pated in any union activities.

Colston:

Well, do you known Susan Quiett?

Scott:

No, but I know her sister.

Colston:

You know, some black people are going around talking about things they don't know anything about.

Scott:

What does that mean?

Colston:

When I worked at the Uniroyal plant, black guys I was working with were on strike, and they didn't even know what they were on strike for. It seems that black people nowadays go around talking about a lot of things they don't know about. Susan's pushing the union, and she doesn't know what she's talking about and she doesn't know anything about the union.

Colston denied having a special conversation with Scott and denied asking her about her union sentiment in the course of any normal conversations.

During mid-January, employee Jacqueline Jones claimed that super-visor David Robertson asked to speak to her and explained that the supervisors were "on a campaign" at that time to find out how the employees felt about the union.

Jones:

What do you mean, "how do I feel about the union?"

Robertson:

Well, some unions are good, some unions want you for your dues, and some unions can really help you. I once worked at Payne and Keller, and they were on strike. They tried to get the union into that.

Jones:

My father worked at Payne and Keller, but I never heard him talk of a strike.

Robertson:

Maybe your father was hired during that strike time. As far as I'm concerned, they never got what they wanted, even though they had strikes.

Robertson denied ever approaching Jones, but admitted that he was instructed to discuss the union campaign with at least five employees. Robertson couldn't recall the instructed content of these discussions.

Around the same time, employee Shirley Trosclair stated that supervisor Gayle Caillouet in nursing services approached her and asked whether she knew anything about the union organizing. When Trosclair replied negatively, Caillouet continued, "Well, if you hear anything, come and contact me. Don't talk to anyone outside, just come to me and talk."

Caillouet admitted that she tried to talk with all of her employees about the union. She had been attending supervisory meetings where the union's strength in various departments was discussed.

The first week of February, employee Ruth Stevenson, along with four other employees, had a conversation with supervisor Nellie Guilbeau:

Guilbeau:

> I'd like to tell you about the union. The union is bad. In my home town, one year a union went on strike and people didn't have food to eat. Some lost their cars and homes. If you go on strike, you aren't guaranteed your jobs once the strike is over. You'd be replaced. And if you have a union, you wouldn't be able to work overtime, adjust your schedule, or come to me with your problems and complaints.

Guilbeau denied telling Stevenson or others that the union was bad. However, she did admit advising Stevenson, and employees in general, that unionization could affect their benefits, such as overtime scheduling and grievance procedures.

In early February, according to Quiett, Colston approached her as she was leaving the cafeteria. Colston asked Quiett what she thought the union could do for her. Quiett responded that the union could give her better working conditions. Colston retorted that the union could also take her job; when the union goes out on strike strikers won't get paid, and the hospital can hire people to replace them.

Colston denies ever approaching Quiett outside the cafeteria. On one occasion, however, Colston claims he saw Quiett crying on the elevator. He asked what was wrong, and Quiett responded, "That's why we need the union in this damn place." No further words were exchanged.

The Speeches

Commencing February 9, 1981, teams of management and supervisory personnel gave a series of speeches to employees in an attempt to dissuade them from union involvement. The text of the speech ran to almost 20 typewritten pages, and management personnel were instructed to follow the text verbatim.

The first of these speeches included a brief statement of objectives, including the declaration that the hospital was "100 percent against

having a union. . . ." Management then went on to explain the procedures for an NLRB election. Next:

Would you like to see a copy of the union contract in the hospital if the union
should win an election here? [Speaker holds up blank sheet of paper.] If the
union should win an election here—and we don't believe that is going to
happen, but just assume for a moment that it did—the hospital would be
obligated to bargain in good faith with the union. That is all. We would do
that bargaining with an intention of reaching an agreement. You should know,
though, that there would be *no automatic* wage increases, *no automatic* benefit
improvements, *no automatic* policies, *no automatic* anything else.

We would start right from this blank sheet of paper, and *not one word, not
one sentence, not one paragraph* would go on that sheet of paper unless the
hospital and the union agreed that it should be on there. Bargaining begins
at the zero point, and *everything* you currently have—your paid holidays, your
wages, your vacations, your hospitalization insurance, your retirement plan—
everything would go on the bargaining table and be subject to the *give* and
take of bargaining.

Under the law, the only thing that the hospital would be required to do,
should the union win the election, is to sit down and bargain in good faith
over your pay and your jobs. We would do that. A union win, however,
would mean an automatic increase in *nothing!* Here is the proof of what I am
saying [holds up a copy of a government leaflet]. Let me read the section
which is circled in red. . . . That's the law and we would obey the law.

Before you think about voting for the union, you need to know *how bargaining works.* You should understand that bargaining can be *cold-blooded* and
impersonal. Nothing is automatic about bargaining between a hospital and a
union. No one knows what will happen or what will come out of bargaining.
The union has made a lot of promises already and will probably be making
more about their getting you more pay, more benefits, and that you will not
have to work so hard. That's the name of the game with unions—promises.
Under the law, there is absolutely no limit on how extravagant promises can
be—the *sky is the limit!*

What would happen if we said NO to the union's demands? What *could*
the union do? What *would* the union do? What could the union do to try to
force us to give in to their demands? There's only one thing that the union
could do to try to force us to give in to their demands and that would be call
you out *on strike*. The *strike* is the *only weapon* that the union has to try to force
the hospital into giving in to its demands—and *you* would be the union's
ammunition.

The speech gives examples of strikers losing pay and being replaced
during a strike, then moves on to give details of deaths and serious
injuries that have occurred during strikes. Finally,

[Hospital president] and [hospital vice president] asked that you discuss
this important matter among yourselves and with your supervisors. If any
union-pusher asks you to vote for the union, demand a *written, signed, notarized*
guarantee that you won't lose your job—that you won't be involved in a strike
or in strike violence. Get it in writing—*demand proof!* You shouldn't take a
chance on the outside union organizer and their strike-happy union. They

have members out of work now, and they are simply looking for someone—you—to make up the money those out-of-work people are no longer paying. Make no mistakes—this whole thing is nothing but a big-money deal for the union and the union's bosses. They plan on taking over, and you are right to figure $100,000 from *you*—*each* and *every* year—if they can get in here and get their hands in your pockets.

Well, that is all we have time to cover today. But if you have any questions or comments about what was covered, feel free to ask those questions or voice those comments. We hope we have cleared up some of the mysteries surrounding what the union can and cannot do. If anytime later you are unsure of something we have covered or something that the union has claimed, we encourage you to ask your supervisor or come by and see another member of management. We want to be sure you get all the *truthful answers* to your questions before this election.

Are there any questions?

Many employees claimed that the speeches given were far stronger than the text above, indicating that the union would strike the hospital, and that employees would lose benefits and/or their jobs if they voted in the union. One employee claimed that Tom Webb's rendition of the speech, in mid-February, contained such threats. A review of hospital personnel records, however, revealed that Webb was not employed after January 30.

EVENTS LEADING TO ALLEGED 8(A)(3) VIOLATIONS

Hamilton

On November 26, Charles Hamilton was called to a conference in George Munn's office. Hamilton was the only assistant chief patient care assistant (PCA) working under Henry Harris, chief PCA.

All PCAs performed a variety of duties, including catheterizing, walking, dressing, and restraining patients. Both Hamilton and Harris spent most of their work week engaged in such duties. In addition, however, Hamilton and Harris assigned jobs throughout the hospital to other PCAs and trained employees, and they occasionally counseled employees on their work performance. On Sundays and Mondays, Harris's days off, Hamilton was in charge of replacing no-show employees, granting employees permission to leave early, dismissing employees early for disciplinary reasons, and even writing up employees for disciplinary action. Hamilton's pay was $1.50 higher than the highest-paid PCA.

Present at the Hamilton meeting were Munn, director of material management; Tom Alexander, hospital vice president; and Harris.

Munn:

Hamilton, I've heard rumors about you being associated with the union, but now I know for a fact after seeing you passing out leaflets.

Alexander:

> Hamilton, are you a union steward?

Hamilton:

> Yes, sir. You could call me that.

Alexander:

> You have a right to your beliefs, but at this point in time I'd like you, as a supervisor, to stand with the hospital on this thing. As a supervisor, you're not eligible to be involved in any union thing. And you know how the hospital feels about the union.

Hamilton:

> Yes, I do.

Alexander:

> As a supervisor, it's your job to uphold the hospital's position 24 hours a day, seven days a week. If you can't do that, then disciplinary action is inevitable.

Later that evening, Harris stopped by Hamilton's house. At that time Hamilton indicated that he had no intention of discontinuing his support of the organizing campaign, even though Harris warned him that continued support would cost him his job.

Wilson

On February 12, 1981, Warner Wilson was called to a meeting in Alexander's office. A washman in the hospital laundry, Wilson, along with three other laundry employees, was designated as a leaderman. His tasks were to load dirty clothes in the washer, send the clothes through the wash cycle, then load them onto a conveyor for further laundry processing. Larry Betz and Gene Miley, Wilson's supervisors, did not work weekends, so Wilson and another leaderman rotated Saturdays. On his Saturdays, Wilson assisted co-workers in getting clothes out and had a phone number to call in the event of an equipment breakdown. If laundry employees came in late or needed other counseling, Wilson was instructed to leave a note on Miley's desk. Wilson, however, had never done this. Although instructed to be sure that he had a full working crew, Wilson was never given a list of employees' phone numbers, so when the laundry was short-handed, he just had the available crew double up. Betz claimed that Wilson had the authority to reprimand employees and grant time off, although he had never explicitly informed Wilson of this authority. Wilson earned $4.98 per hour.

Persons present at the Wilson conference included Alexander, Betz, and another supervisor, Bill Snider.

Alexander:

> We just got the result of who was eligible to vote yesterday. You are a supervisor and you are under management; therefore, you are not eligible to vote.

Wilson:

> If I'm a supervisor, how come I'm not drawing supervisor's pay?

Alexander:

> You'll have to take that up with Miley. You are a supervisor. You are not allowed to vote. I don't want you to say anything or speak up for the union. I don't want you to discuss the union with anyone, or it could mean your job. I personally called you up here to tell you not to discuss anything about the union, because it could mean your job. Do you understand what I mean?

Wilson:

> I understand exactly what you mean.

A few days later, Betz had another conversation with Wilson. Betz warned Wilson that "they are out to get you—they are out to get your job." Wilson replied that as long as he put in his eight hours, he had nothing to worry about. Wilson, along with Hamilton and 52 other employees, was laid off on February 20, 1981.

The hospital cited the February layoffs as part of a reduction-in-force planned due to declining patient census. In May 1980, the hospital's staff-to-patient ratio was significantly above the acceptable level of 3.3 to 3.6 employees per patient. Despite attrition over the next several months, the hospital's December 1980 level was still too high. Hospital vice president Edward Silvey advised Joyce Burkeen, director of nursing services, to lay off 20 nurses' aides; Melda Pace, head of housekeeping, to lay off four employees; and he ordered various other layoffs throughout the hospital.

Of the 20 nurses' aides laid off, 5 were known union activists. The names of Booker, LaCour, and Thomas were on the union's organizing committee list sent to management in late November. Management had seen Stevenson handbilling during early February. Wilson claimed that a supervisor interrogated her regarding her union sentiment prior to the layoff announcement. Two of the four maids laid off, Jones and Quiett, had been observed handbilling and had engaged in numerous conversations with various supervisors regarding their union activity. Wilson was the only laundryman laid off; Hamilton was the only PCA.

Nursing's Layoff Selection Process.   In order to determine which 20 nurses' aides to layoff, Burkeen discussed all aides' performances with their supervisors and reviewed all personnel records. This process revealed 40 aides with outstanding performance records. The remaining 68 were ranked according to records of their absenteeism and tardiness during the past year. Three of the 23 nurses' aides with the worst records were given consideration due to special circumstances.

Those three included one aide that was receiving workers' compensation benefits after contracting hepatitis at the hospital. Another was an employee who frequently worked back-to-back shifts (16 hours), and would then be late returning for her next scheduled shift eight hours later. The third with special circumstances was a nursing student who encountered conflicts between her work and class schedules. The hospital agreed to this sporadic absenteeism with the understanding that the aide would be hired following her graduation as a registered nurse. Booker, LaCour, Thomas, Stevenson, and Wilson were among the remaining 20 nurses' aides with the most frequent occurrences of absenteeism and tardiness .

Housekeeping's Layoff Selection Process.   Pace utilized the number of disciplinary offenses over the past year as the basis for layoff decisions. Quiett and another maid, Thompson, had the most offenses at five each; Jones had four; the fourth laid-off maid, Tate, had three. Exhibit 1 (see p. 13) outlines Quiett's and Jones's offenses.

Laundry's Layoff Selection Process.   Miley contended that it was necessary to lay off one leaderman. The basis for the selection of Wilson was his lack of seniority. While Wilson was the most junior leaderman on the day shift, he had seniority over another leaderman on the night shift. Wilson, however, was not given an opportunity to transfer to the night shift to avoid being laid off.

Hamilton was the only PCA laid off. No explanation of the selection process for this decision was provided.

ELECTION RESULTS

On May 7, 1981, the SEIU lost their certification election at Baton Rouge General Hospital: of the 915 employees voting, only 276 voted for the union.

QUESTION

As a union advocate, what occurrences are the basis for your allegations against Baton Rouge General Hospital? What defenses to these allegations do you think management will propose?

Exhibit   **13**

EXHIBIT 1   Conference Reports of Quiett and Jones

Date	Offense
Quiett	
May 28, 1980	Smoking
July 16, 1980	Verbal warning
December 7, 1980	Overstaying break
December 8, 1980	Absenteeism counseling*
Jones	
September 16, 1980	Not reporting for work
September 20, 1980	Overstaying break
December 5, 1980	Insubordination
December 16, 1980	Absenteeism counseling†

*Over the past year Quiett had been late 12 times, ill nine times, absent nine times, and had an illness in her family 15 times. In addition, Quiett was on maternity leave from January 26 through April 8, 1980; on surgery leave August 24 through October 27, 1980.

†Over the past year Jones had been late 32 times, ill 17 times, absent seven times, and had an illness in her family four times.

Market King and the United Food and Commercial Workers Union

On October 21, 1982, a former Kroger store located in Monterey Park, California, opened as Market King under the ownership of William Chu and family. The store offered an expanded line of ethnic foods and was staffed with 20 new employees, none of whom had worked for Kroger. Former Kroger employees, represented by the Food and Commercial Workers Union Local 770, picketed the store. The workers passed out leaflets urging patrons to shop at unionized supermarkets, claiming that the successor ownership refused to bargain in good faith with the incumbent union.

On November 11, an article regarding the dispute appeared in a local Chinese community newspaper. In the article, Chu stated that hiring union members would increase costs for the store, which he could not afford as an independent owner. A political science professor from a nearby university offered to mediate the dispute, but Chu declined. As a result, picketing and leaflet distribution continued. The union filed Section 8(a)(5) charges with the regional office of the National Labor Relations Board on December 7, 1982 and March 14, 1983. Chu filed a lawsuit against Kroger seeking to rescind the purchase and sale agreement. On July 1, 1983, Market King filed a petition Chapter 11, signed by Chu, with the U.S. Bankruptcy Court for the Central District of California.

---

*This case was based upon a January 1987 National Labor Relations Board Decision.

THE COMMUNITY

Monterey Park, located seven miles east of Los Angeles, is a small, divergent, middle-income community (see Exhibit 1, p. 19). In the early 1800s the area was part of the Mission of San Gabriel de Arcangel and was populated predominantly by white and Spanish-surnamed settlers. Monterey Park became a city in 1916, in an effort to block the neighboring cities' attempts to develop a large sewage plant in the area. By 1920 a large Asian farming population had migrated to the area. Although the depression slowed population growth, a series of commercial and residential annexations increased the population fourfold during the 40s and 50s. Today Monterey Park is a self-sufficient commercial community with numerous industries (see Exhibit 2, p. 20).

THE SALE OF THE MARKET BASKET STORES

Until 1982, the Kroger Company of Cincinnati, Ohio, owned and operated 63 stores in southern California under the name of Market Basket. As a member of a multiemployer bargaining group, the Food Employers' Council, Kroger recognized the United Food and Commercial Workers International Union (UFCWU), Local 770, as collective bargaining representative of retail grocery clerks employed at store number 113 in Monterey Park. Local 770's contract, effective July 27, 1981 through July 29, 1984, was one of three union contracts covering store 113.[1]

During 1982, Kroger advertised and sold the individual stores of the Market Basket chain to other chains and independent operators. In the event of a store's sale, the Food Employers' Council's agreement with Local 770 contained the following provision:

Article XVIII
Successors and Assigns

B. NEW OWNER.

This Agreement shall be binding upon the successors and assigns of the parties hereto. In the event of bona fide sale or transfer of any store covered by this Agreement during the period hereof, the new owner or such transferee shall be notified of the obligation of this Agreement and be required to become a party hereto. The former owner shall be required to meet any and all monetary benefits that employees have accumulated under this Agreement.

*   *   *   *   *

---

[1]The council also had agreements with the Bakery and Confectionary Workers' Union, expiring February 28, 1985, and the UFCW Meat Cutters' Union, expiring November 1982.

D. SALE OR TRANSFER

1. In the event of a sale or transfer of a store or stores, an employee shall be allowed a seven (7) day period from the date of announcement to the employees of the sale or transfer during which time s/he may determine whether s/he wishes to stay with the seller or whether s/he wishes to make application for employment with the new owner or transferee. In the event the employee chooses to remain with the seller, such choice shall not be construed as any guarantee of employment over and beyond the terms of this Agreement.

2. In the event of a sale or transfer of a store or stores, the new owner or transferee shall make every effort to fill employment needs in such a store or stores from those employees of the seller or transferor who were employed in the stores sold or transferred.

3. Such new owner or transferee, however, shall not be required to retain in his employ any of the employees of the seller or transferor.

William Chu telephoned a Kroger official in mid-July of 1982, expressing interest in purchasing two Market Basket stores, including store number 113 in Monterey Park. Chu, a licensed real estate broker since 1979, had executed over 100 residential purchases and sales agreements. Moreover, Chu had also owned and sold a cocktail lounge and restaurant and served as an officer of a Los Angeles investment company.

Following Chu's telephone call, Kroger's real estate director forwarded three copies of the standard sales agreement to Chu, listing the agreed-upon price of $200,000 per store. The sales price included Kroger's inventory, equipment, liquor license, and other assets.

At a meeting the following week in Los Angeles, Chu told the real estate director that he was now only interested in purchasing one store, number 113. Chu also expressed concern over assuming the union contracts per paragraph 5 of the sales agreement (see Exhibit 3, p. 21), stating that independent operators couldn't bear the cost of such contracts. Kroger's real estate director indicated that the company was bound by law to include paragraph 5, but that their labor relations department would meet with the union and seek contract concessions for the smaller operators.

In early August, Chu returned the executed purchase and sales agreement to Kroger, but had crossed out paragraph 5. The real estate director telephoned Chu, indicating that any store transfer must include paragraph 5. Following the conversation, the director forwarded to Chu new pages for the ones crossed out.

In mid-August, Chu visited the store with William Kwan, Market King's intended vice president. Chu and Kwan approached one employee about remaining on as store manager. The employee asked whether Market King would be unionized, to which Chu replied, "No, we cannot afford it."

Around August 23, Chu again contacted Kroger, again contesting paragraph 5. Over an office speaker phone, four Kroger officials discussed the paragraph, as well as the unsuccessful meeting with the union regarding independent-operator concessions. Chu suggested that, being forced to assume union contract liability, he should be granted a discount in the store sales price. After some negotiation, Kroger agreed to reduce the price by $12,500; instructed Chu to change and initial the new sales price on his copy of the agreement; and to initial pages two and three of the sales agreement pertaining to paragraph 5. Chu then requested copies of the labor contracts that he was assuming.

Chu signed the altered and initialed purchase and sales agreement August 24 and returned the agreement to Kroger. On August 26, Kroger's real estate director forwarded copies of the labor agreement to Chu per Chu's earlier request. On August 31, Kroger's legal department approved the purchase and sales agreement, and Kroger countersigned.

Later, Chu denied that the reduction in sales price was the quid pro quo for paragraph 5. According to Chu, the sales price reduction was the result of earlier negotiation with Kroger officials, during the time Chu discussed purchasing two stores. Kroger offered a $25,000 discount for the purchase of two stores; when Chu decided to purchase only one, he requested a discount of $12,500. Regarding the August 23 telephone conversation, Chu insisted that Kroger claimed that paragraph 5 was merely a formality. But for this oral representation, contended Chu, he would not have signed the purchase and sales agreement. This argument formed the basis of Chu's lawsuit to rescind the purchase and sales agreement.

In late August, Chu again visited the store. An employee asked whether Chu intended to retain any current employees. Chu responded, "Yes, most likely if the union goes the way we want them to."

On September 1, Chu filed articles of incorporation for Market King, Inc. with the state of California, listing Chu as president, a director, the majority stockholder, and agent for process service. Chu's wife was also listed as a stockholder and director; Chu's mother was listed as a stockholder. Chu's real estate and investment company office was listed as Market King's principal place of business.

On September 3, management consultants hired by Chu met with the union representative to discuss the current contract terms. Also present at the meeting were Chu, William Kwan, and two other associates of Chu. While the union representative rejected the specific proposals presented by the consultants, he expressed interest in further negotiations. Another meeting was set for September 8. Prior to the scheduled meeting, the consultants called the union representative to cancel, indicating that Chu had decided against purchasing the store. That same day, however, the union received formal notice from Kroger regarding the execution of the Kroger-Chu sales agreement. The union representative called Kroger's industrial relations director on September 9 to confirm that Chu had purchased the store as a full successor to the collective bargaining agreement. Kroger operated the store through September 11, at which time all employees were laid off or terminated pending transfer.

Chu did not obtain possession of the store until October 11 due to a disagreement with the building lessor. However, between September 15 and September 30, Chu advertised for experienced employees in a Monterey Park newspaper, listing his real estate office telephone number and Kwan's name. The advertisement contained no reference as to the store name or location. According to Chu, Market King was expanding the Latino and Oriental food section to cater to the community's ethnic population, so bilingual ability in either Spanish or Chinese dialects was an employment requirement. On the application were questions regarding an applicant's fluency in any foreign languages, preceded by the statement: "Do not answer the following questions unless specifically directed to do so." On September 15 and 22, Chu interviewed applicants at his real estate office. The store opened for business on October 21.

Between September 22, 1982, and January 26, 1983, former Kroger employees, all union members, applied or attempted to apply for employment at Market King (see Exhibit 4, p. 22). While filing applications, several were asked whether they knew that the store would be nonunion. One employee, Crandall, called the store in early October and spoke with Chu. After identifying herself as a former Market Basket employee, Crandall claims Chu stated, "I am going nonunion. . . . [b]ecause I am Chinese . . . Chinese ways are different from American . . . I want to run the store different." When Crandall arrived at the store for an application form, she was informed that they didn't have any. On October 18, when Ming picked up an application, he was informed that all positions had been filled by family and friends. No former Kroger employees were hired. When the store opened its doors on October 21, the grand opening was attended by numerous union picketers.

QUESTIONS

1. What was Chu's duty to bargain in good faith with Local 770?
2. How would bankruptcy affect this duty?

EXHIBIT 1 Monterey Park Demographics (population 58,582)

Ethnic Characteristics			*Education Levels*	
Hispanic	37	%	Elementary	14.6%
Caucasian	22		High School (1–3)	13.1
Chinese	20		High School (4)	30.0
Japanese	4		College (1–3)	21.3
Vietnamese	4		College (4)	21.0
Taiwanese	4			
Filipino	4			
Korean	2			
Thai	2			
Black	1			

Age Characteristics		*Income After Taxes*	
Under 10	13.1%	$10,000–14,999	8.1%
10–20 years	16.2	$15,000–24,999	28.6
20–24 years	9.8	$25,000–49,999	47.8
25–34 years	17.1	$50,000+	15.5
35–44 years	11.5		
45–54 years	11.9		
55–64 years	11.0		
over 64	9.4		

EXHIBIT 2   Monterey Park Employment Data (total labor force = 26,835;
unemployment = 4.5%)

Industry*	Percent Employment
Manufacturing	20.5%
General business	18.8
Retail trade	17.4
Eductional services	8.9
Health services	7.5
Transportation, communication, utilities	7.3
Wholesale trade	6.2
Public administration	5.7
Construction	3.0
Other	4.7

Major Area Employers	Number of Employees
East Los Angeles College	1,800
Garfield Medical Center	604
Ameron, Inc.	504
Lloyd's Bank	400
C.F. Braun & Co.	350
Monterey Park Hospital	325
City of Monterey Park	311
Carolyn Shoes, Inc.	260
Merchants Building Maintenance & Guard	210
Colours	200
Oltmans Construction Co.	200
Dun & Bradstreet	199
Autographics, Inc.	150
Leegin Creative Leather, Inc.	100

*Extent of unionization: The majority of industries are highly unionized; a smaller group operates under union contracts; a very small number have a very limited union affiliation.

EXHIBIT 3   Kroger's Standard Purchase and Sale Agreement

Paragraph 5: Assumption of Liabilities

(a) Purchaser shall assume as of the Closing Date, and perform when due, Seller's obligations arising after the Closing under the Contracts and the Leases(s) pertaining to the Store(s) purchased. (b) Seller, as a member of the Southern California Food Employees' Council, Inc., is a party to various labor contracts covering the Store(s) which are described herein . . . :

Purchaser agrees to become a successor to all of said applicable contracts and to abide by all relevant terms of conditions thereof including the employment of Seller's bargaining unit employees in accordance with said contracts.

Seller will, however, defend and hold Purchaser harmless for any grievances or claims filed and relating to Purchaser's operations of the involved Store(s) prior to the Closing. Purchaser shall defend and hold Seller harmless for any such claims arising out of its operations subsequent to Closing.

Further, Purchaser agrees to contribute to the multi-employer pension plan(s) listed . . . for those employees who are currently participants in said plan(s) and who are retained and employed by Purchaser in accordance with the terms and conditions of the labor agreement(s) listed. . . .

Purchaser will also provide to each of the plan(s) listed . . . for a period of five plan-years commencing with the first plan-year after the day of this sale, a bond or the equivalent security, either of which must be acceptable to Seller, in an amount equal to the greater of: (a) the average annual contribution required to be made by the Seller with respect to the involved operations and plan(s) for the three (3) plan-years preceding the plan-year in which the sale of the operations occurred; (b) the annual contribution that the Seller was required to make with respect to the involved operations and plan(s) for the last plan-year before the plan-year in which the sale of the operations occurred.

Seller agrees to be secondarily liable to the described plans for any withdrawal liability required by law to be paid which arises out of Purchaser's withdrawal from said plan(s) during the said first five (5) plan-years.

EXHIBIT 4   Former Kroger Employees Seeking Employment At Market King

Date	Employee*	Response
9/17	Anthony Penoro	"Not hiring"
9/22	Theresa Marsala	Applied but was not hired
10/08	Sue Crandall	No applications
10/13	Mark Forni	Applied but was not hired
10/14	Maria Garcia	Applied but was not hired
	David Smith	Applied but was not hired
	Jesus Ricardo	Applied but was not hired
10/19	Joey Ming	Applied but was not hired
	Myra Castillo	Applied but was not hired
	Beth Langley	Applied but was not hired
10/21	Eric Simpson	No applications
	Dan Haffrey	No applications
	Bill Campbell	No applications
10/22	Renee Sanco	Applied but was not hired
10/28	Jerry Golden	Applied but was not hired
01/26/83	Matt Hyatt	Applied but was not hired

*Names are fictitious.

Contract Negotiations

Primo Plastic, Inc. and the Associated Rubber and Plastics Specialty Workers

Negotiations between Primo Plastic's Junction Falls plant and Associated Rubber and Plastics Specialty Workers (ARPSW) Local 488 begin next month. Junction Falls is one of three Primo Plastic facilities which manufacture a variety of injection-molded plastic components and containers for the consumer and commercial packaged goods industry. Two facilities are unionized; one is not. The company remains adamant about keeping negotiations at the two unionized facilities separate despite similarity in production processes.

Management, in the face of Primo Plastic's decreasing market share, claims efficiency, capital expenditures, productivity, and product quality must increase within and across their three plants. The company's rumored pending plant closure at Toledo, however, and expansion of operations at the nonunion Breezie Hill plant clearly concern the Junction Falls ARPSW members. Moreover, in 1986 the company attempted to subcontract out much of the work performed by Junction Falls' finishing department. As a result, public statements by union leaders (especially from the ARPSW district and regional offices) strongly suggests that Local 488 will focus on contract provisions that protect members' job and income security.

THE PACKAGING INDUSTRY

The U.S. packaging market is a $70 billion-a-year industry involving producers of cardboard/paper, metal, glass, and plastic containers. The plastic segment of this industry is by far the strongest, growing at a rate of over 10 percent annually. This growth, initially cannibalized from glass and metal containers, is now fueled by the use of plastic packaging for microwaveable food products. Despite this growth, keen competition stabilized prices.

Historically, mostly small companies produced miscellaneous plastic products:

1985 Total Assets	Percent of Companies
Under $250,000	44
$250,000–$1 million	31
$1 million–$5 million	18
Over $5 million	7

However, several large metal and glass producers, including Aluminum Company of America (ALCOA), General Electric Plastics, Dorsey Corporation, and Continental Can Company, recently announced multi-million-dollar allocations for the research, development, and production of new plastics lines.

These new big-company entrants concern the smaller producers. Industry profits are highly leveraged by competitive pricing coupled with the need for heavy R&D expenditures. Larger companies invest heavily in future projects, winning great favor among the industry's customers. Moreover, many smaller companies now experience difficulty bidding competitively for raw materials. This situation is exacerbated by an industry shortage of polyethylene terephthalate (PET) packaging resins, with larger companies garnishing priority shipments of the material.

Furthermore, the growth in the use of plastics resulted in the passage of new environmental laws that sharply curbed traditional disposal methods. The feasibility of recycling the material is still being tested, and there is speculation that environmentalists will lobby for government limits on yearly production.

COMPANY BACKGROUND

Primo Plastic, Inc. was founded in 1970 by Robert Sullivan and Larry Prince. Sullivan and Prince were graduate students at the University of Michigan's Graduate School of Business Administration from 1968 through 1970. Before entering the M.B.A. program, Sullivan earned a B.S. degree in chemical engineering from Purdue University and worked for several years for a large midwestern chemical company. Prince earned a B.S. degree in economics from Ohio State University and worked for a short time as a staff consultant in an oil company.

Sullivan and Prince first met while summer interns in production operations at a large East Coast packaged goods manufacturer. Their summer experience was extremely frustrating as they were continually barraged with marketing's demands for package variations coinciding with promotions. It seemed that suppliers couldn't meet deadlines, shipped poor-quality product, or didn't have sufficient line capacity to meet the demand of the more successful promotions. The result: sales managers screamed, brand managers screamed, and the suppliers' sales staff were invariably out of the office. Sullivan and Prince decided that an efficient specialty plastics container supplier would garner large and loyal contracts.

The second year in their M.B.A. program, Sullivan and Prince stumbled upon a failing Toledo plastics molding company while researching an operations management case. They toured the facility and afterwards spent considerable time getting price estimates on new and used injection molding equipment. Pooling savings, borrowing money from their parents, and securing financing, they purchased the facility for the value of its existing assets. By selling off unneeded equipment and using personal lines of credit, Sullivan and Prince then secured enough capital to convert the remaining equipment.

The Toledo facility had been unionized by Local 230 of the Associated Rubber and Plastics Specialty Workers (ARPSW) several years before. At the time of purchase, labor costs were approximately 10 percent above the industry average and 15 percent above the Toledo labor market. In less than two years, Sullivan and Prince made the first Primo Plastic facility highly profitable without seeking concessions from Local 230, but by aggressively target marketing their product line with the slogan: "Excellence, On-Time, or Free." The company enjoyed modest, but steady growth. Primo Plastic expanded by building the Junction Falls facility in 1974, and the Breezie Hill facility in 1984.

During the last several years, however, the company's well-being has fluctuated with materials shortages and increasing competition from large domestic newcomers. In addition, many customers are vertically integrating container production. Although Primo Plastic's market share increased from 3 percent in 1971 to 8 percent today, national media attention to the industry mergers and acquisitions has everyone concerned as to whether a small company like Primo Plastic can survive.

UNION BACKGROUND

The Associated Rubber and Plastic Specialty Workers (ARPSW) is an international union composed of 278 locals in 43 states, Puerto Rico, and Canada. Most of their organized companies are small, employing between 75 and 1,000 workers. Over the past decade, however, the number of successful organizing attempts declined by almost 25 percent. Thus, every new company organized, regardless of size, is important to the International.

International President, J. W. Curry, elected in 1970, remains one of labor's most respected champions. He personally made the ARPSW into a viable organization. Before enrolling in Case Western Law School, he successfully organized Local 242 in Englewood Heights, New Jersey, and served as Local president for five years. Graduating at the top of his law school class, Curry then joined the International's legal staff. Within a short time, Curry was appointed ARPSW general counsel. Elected as an ARPSW vice president in 1964, he soon earned a reputation as a highly dedicated and savvy negotiator and organizer.

Despite Curry's reputation, union growth slowed, and some younger leaders felt his approach was too soft. There has been no significant strike activity for several years, with Curry favoring a more cooperative approach. The loss of Breezie Hill in 1986 reignited dissent within the union.

Rick Chapman, elected district director by a convention of local unions in southern Illinois in 1976, is credited with the successful organization of Primo Plastic's Junction Falls facility by Local 488 in 1979. This was an important achievement for the ARPSW since Junction Falls is located in the heart of a largely unorganized area. Chapman received substantial assistance from International representative Nancy Schuman, at the time director of organizing. Schuman joined the International following graduation from Cornell in 1968, starting as an assistant to the research director. Schuman spent substantial time in the field collecting data on organizing activities and became increasingly empathetic to the frustrations of local union leaders. Schuman is now regional director of the region that includes Local 488 and has the largest ARPSW penetration. Both Schuman and Chapman have emerged as key critics of International's "soft solidarity." As Curry approaches retirement, their criticism becomes more pointed, more public, and more frequent. While not directly involved in the upcoming negotiations, both Schuman and Chapman are actively involved with members of the union negotiating team.

Local 488 is run by an elected executive committee that includes recently elected president Wade Griffith, the vice president, the secretary-treasurer, and three committee persons. The executive committee meets weekly to listen to reports of the shop stewards and to take up the business necessary to run the union.

Griffith works full time as a lead maintenance mechanic at Primo Plastic and was chief steward at Junction Falls prior to becoming Local president. Nicknamed Andy (after actor Andy Griffith) by his co-workers because of his even, good-natured personality, Griffith has negotiated several contracts.

Griffith surprised many people by appointing Bob Adler chief steward; many view Adler as a troublemaker and opportunist. During the last round of negotiations, Adler was rumored to have let the air out of the tires of several company trucks. However, he has a strong following among the younger workers in the plant. Griffith and Adler would be the key union participants in the upcoming negotiations.

LABOR-MANAGEMENT HISTORY

Toledo. Primo Plastic-Toledo prospered throughout the 1970s despite severe oil shortages and resultant raw material shortages of 1973–74. Employees continued enjoying above-average wages and benefits, as Sullivan and Prince aggressively pursued new, price inelastic markets. The early 80s recession took its toll, however, and prices flattened. As the economy recovered, the new, larger competitors entered the market; prices remained lower than expected. Employment grew from 225 in 1970 to a high of 580 in 1981, but steady cutbacks since 1981 have reduced employment in the Toledo plant to its current level of 340 production and maintenance workers.

Primo Plastic management requested substantial concessions from Local 230 at the Toledo plant during 1984 negotiations, concessions "necessary to justify major capital expenditures in an aging facility." Furthermore, the labor cost differential between Junction Hills and Toledo grew to about 12 percent, as the reduction in force at Toledo left an older, better-compensated workforce than at the Junction Falls plant. Local 230 responded that management had always expanded their market share within the growing plastic packaging industry, so major concessions weren't necessary. The union accepted a two-year wage freeze in exchange for a $750 lump-sum first-year payment.

Shortly after signing the contract, management announced there would be no capital expenditures or expansion of employment at Toledo. In fact, as stated by Primo Plastic's vice president of production, "Although not necessarily through attrition, Primo Plastic intends decreasing plant utilization [at Toledo] in favor of those facilities with more cooperative labor-management relations." The following year, Primo Plastic announced plans for a new production facility in Breezie Hill, Tennessee.

Junction Falls (site of the upcoming negotiations). In contrast to the Toledo facility, the Junction Falls plant has experienced steady market share and employment growth since it was built in 1974.

ARPSW Local 488 was certified by the NLRB as the exclusive representative of all production and maintenance workers at the Junction Falls facility in 1979. The ARPSW won the election with 62 percent of the workers voting for representation. The election campaign became very heated in the final weeks of the campaign, resulting in the filing of an election objection by the company, charging the union with campaign misrepresentation of company profitability. The NLRB Regional Office dismissed Primo Plastic's campaign objection and certified Local 488.

After eight months of difficult negotiations accompanied by a one-week strike, Primo Plastic signed an 18-month agreement with Local 488. Although the ARPSW sought to negotiate wages and benefits equal to Local 230 at Toledo, direct labor compensation at Junction Falls remained 9 percent below labor costs at the Toledo plant.

In 1982 Primo Plastic and Local 488 signed a three-year agreement, with ARPSW obtaining modest wage and benefit increases. The union negotiated hard for a cost of living adjustment (COLA), but reluctantly withdrew that demand in lieu of improved health and welfare benefits.

During 1985 negotiations, management emphasized that the newly opened Breezie Hill facility's direct labor compensation was 6 percent lower and productivity already 10 to 15 percent higher than at Junction Falls. As a result, corporate headquarters intended to expand production at Breezie Hill. Management would, however, "attempt further capital investment and facility expansion at Junction Falls if compensation were controlled. Nor would Primo Plastic be opposed to exploring the highly successful employee involvement activities such as were brought on board at Breezie Hill, and believed to be a major source of the labor savings realized at that facility."

In December 1985, the company and union signed another three-year agreement at Junction Falls, with no improvement in benefits and relatively modest wage gains. Both parties also signed a memorandum of agreement to develop a joint steering committee charged with developing an employee involvement program.

At the present time, Junction Falls' employment remains at the 1986 level, and capital expenditures are predominantly for machine replacement. Despite the memorandum of agreement, the joint steering committee never rallied sufficient support from either management or the union to proceed with any programs. One exception to this followed management's 1986 subcontracting announcement. Amid considerable animosity, the joint steering committee was granted six months to find an acceptable alternative to subcontracting out much of the work performed by the finishing department. Later hailed by many as an important effort at joint problem solving, the ad hoc committee recommended utilizing some new technologies and performing major repair work in-house (the latter generally being contracted out). This redesign of the finishing process reduced costs by 16 percent; the subcontracting bid reduced costs by only 14 percent. Only two finishers were displaced following implementation of the committee's recommendations.

Breezie Hill (nonunion).   Breezie Hill currently employs 340 production and maintenance workers and recently announced further expansion plans. Breezie Hill management remains emphatic that it will strongly resist unionization of the plant. By instigating quality circles and a Scanlonlike gainsharing arrangement, worker interest in union representation seems minimal. In fact, the ARPSW lost its bid for representation in October 1986 when 68 percent of the work force voted against representation in a NLRB-conducted certification election.

BASIC TERMS OF CONTRACT

Health and Welfare Benefits

Group life insurance is paid in full by Primo Plastic. Workers are eligible after one month of service, with the benefit level set at 1.5 times an employee's annual wage. The company also provides sickness and accident coverage for a maximum of 26 weeks, equivalent to 65 percent of an employee's annual wage. After one month of service, an employee is eligible for sickness and accident coverage, which the company pays at 100 percent of coverage costs.

Long-term disability (LTD) benefits are provided in full by the company, equal to 60 percent of an employee's annual wage. Employees are eligible for LTD benefits after two months of service and qualify for benefits after 26 weeks of disability.

Comprehensive medical coverage is provided in full by the company. Primo Plastic also pays for 80 percent of coverage costs for dependents. The plan includes a $100 deductible for employees and a $200 deductible for dependents, with a $10,000 annual maximum in benefits to employees and a $5,000 annual maximum per dependent.

Pension Benefits

After one year of service, employees become eligible for an ERISA-qualified defined pension plan. Plan contributions are made exclusively by the company. The annual annuity upon retirement at age 65, with 10 years service, is equal to 1.5 percent of the employee's last five years average annual earnings, multiplied by years of service.

Vacations

Employees with greater than one or less than three years of continuous service receive a one-week vacation. After three years of service, employees receive two weeks of vacation; and after 15 years of service employees receive three weeks of vacation. It is estimated that costs are reduced by one percentage point each year of the contract due to turnover.

Holidays

Holidays recognized are New Year's Day, Washington's Birthday, Memorial Day, Independence Day, Labor Day, Thanksgiving, Veterans Day, and Christmas. Holidays falling on Saturday are celebrated on Friday; holidays falling on Sunday are celebrated on Monday. Employees are paid their straight-time hourly rate if they were on pay status the work days preceding and following the holiday. Employees required to work are paid straight time plus pay for the holiday. Employees on average work 1.5 holidays per year.

CURRENT NEGOTIATION ISSUES

Primo Plastic's tough stand at Toledo and rumors of a pending plant closure there alarm many ARPSW members. In addition, the ARPSW believes that the Breezie Hill plant's nonunion status and planned expansion pose a serious threat to job security. Although the finishing department work remained within the Junction Falls facility, the subcontracting threat certainly angered several union activists.

Word is that union leaders' demands will include:

1. Contract provisions giving Junction Falls workers transfer rights to Breezie Hill.
2. Restrictions on subcontracting.
3. More protective layoff and recall rights.
4. Severance pay.
5. Supplemental unemployment benefits (SUB).

Furthermore, Local 488 president Griffith seemingly seeks top dollar in wages; other union representatives want provisions for a COLA, paid sick leave, and personal paid holidays. At a recent local union meeting following discussion of changes in ERISA's vesting provisions, there was also considerable interest expressed in changing the pension vesting provision to graded vesting after three years of service. Finally, there has been significant grumbling among the rank and file that the distribution of overtime has not been equitable and that the contract language allows supervisors to reward their friends.

Junction Falls management indicates that a wage freeze would enable financing of further capital expenditures (presumably at the Junction Falls facility) and equalize compensation with the Breezie Hill plant. In addition, management officials have been discussing ways to increase personnel efficiency via greater management discretion in work assignments across job classifications. Management's early reaction to providing Local 488 members with transfer rights to their nonunion Breezie Hill facility and to allowing the ARPSW to place restrictions on subcontracting can be characterized as "noncompromising." Finally, some key management officials want Local 488 and the company to jointly implement programs on productivity and quality improvement.

Exhibits 1–11, which follow, provide detailed financial and labor-management information on Primo Plastic. The agreement between Primo Plastic and the ARPSW is presented in Appendix I (see p. 46).

EXHIBIT 1   Primo Plastic, Inc.—Junction Falls, Statement of Income

	Fiscal Year Ended		
	Sept. 30, 1987	*Sept. 30, 1986*	*Sept. 30, 1985*
Sales:	$16,035,069	$15,572,914	$14,724,740
Costs of goods sold	12,575,638	12,260,856	11,556,406
Gross profit	3,459,431	3,312,058	3,168,334
Operating expenses	1,526,177	1,482,512	1,440,870
Operating income:	1,933,254	1,829,546	1,727,464
Interest expense	208,455	233,594	194,222
Other expense (income) net	(18,200)	1,360	(14,670)
Income before taxes	1,742,999	1,594,592	1,547,912
Taxes	389,900	379,002	342,669
Net income	$ 1,353,099	$ 1,215,590	$ 1,205,243

EXHIBIT 2   Primo Plastic, Inc.—Junction Falls, Balance Sheet,
September 30, 1987

ASSETS

Current assets:

Cash	$ 3,329,374	
Net receivables	4,069,234	
Inventories:		
Finished goods	2,589,513	
Production materials	1,479,722	
Prepaid expenses	369,930	
Total current assets		$11,837,772
Property, Plant, and Equipment:		
Land, buildings, equipment	7,213,643	
Accumulated depreciation	(2,219,583)	
Net		$ 4,994,060
Investments	1,664,687	
Total assets		$18,496,520

LIABILITIES

Current liabilities:

Short-term debt	$ 462,414	
Accounts payable	2,219,582	
Accrued liabilities	2,034,617	
Income taxes payable	370,436	
Total current liabilities		$ 5,087,049
Long-term debt:		
Mortgage payable	2,589,513	
Deferred income taxes	1,369,424	
Total liabilities		$ 9,045,985
Shareholders' equity:		
Capital stock	1,572,205	
Retained earnings	7,878,330	
Total liabilities and shareholder equity		$18,496,520

EXHIBIT 3   Primo Plastic/Junction Falls Shop Organization

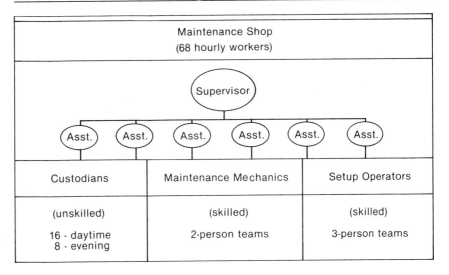

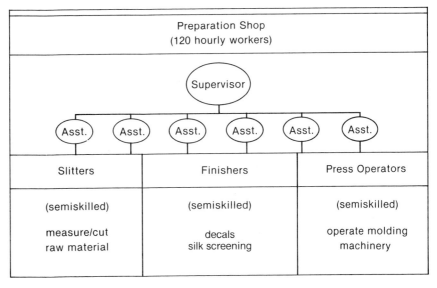

EXHIBIT   3—*Concluded*

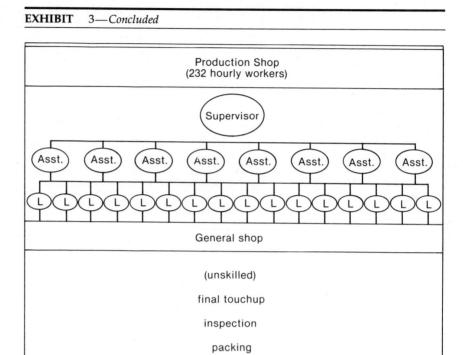

Note: Within the production shop, 140 workers are female.
   Asst. = Assistant supervisor.
   L   = Line leader (all male).

EXHIBIT 4 Employment and Wage Chronology and Current Years of Service

Job Classification	Number of Employees				Wage Rate				Years of Service, December 1987														
	1983	1985	1986	1987	1983	1985	1986	1987	<½	<1	1	2	3	4	5	6	7	8	9	10	11	12
Setup operators	26	26	26	26	$9.96	$10.46	$11.09	$11.48	0	0	0	0	4	2	0	1	2	3	4	3	3	4
Maintenance mechanics	20	19	18	18	9.42	9.89	10.48	10.85	0	0	1	2	2	0	1	0	0	4	1	3	2	2
Press operators	40	40	40	40	8.88	9.33	9.89	10.24	0	0	0	2	7	12	6	4	2	3	0	2	1	1
Slitters	26	25	24	24	8.77	9.21	9.76	10.10	0	1	2	2	3	2	4	5	2	2	1	0	0	0
Finishers	60	57	58	56	8.64	9.08	9.62	9.90	1	2	10	6	10	7	5	8	3	2	1	1	0	0
General shop workers	247	225	235	232	8.46	8.87	9.42	9.75	2	10	31	26	49	26	24	12	16	9	11	7	5	4
Custodians	26	25	24	24	7.81	8.20	8.69	9.00	1	1	5	5	5	0	2	3	0	0	1	0	0	1

Exhibit 5   Weighted Average Labor Costs per Hour Paid

Year	Hourly Wage Rate	Overtime	Health and Welfare	Holiday Pay*	Vacation Pay	Pension	Statutory	Total
1983	$8.64	$.238	$1.242	$.293	$.147	$ .950	$1.037	$12.547
1985	9.07	.250	1.350	.328	.181	.998	1.088	13.265
1986	9.61	.265	1.434	.349	.212	1.057	1.153	14.080
1987	9.95	.275	1.578	.364	.322	1.095	1.194	14.788

*Holiday pay calculations include costs of holidays worked, which has averaged approximately 1.5 holidays per year per employee.

Exhibit 6 Input-Output Financial Statement

| Year | Bargaining Unit Employees | Other Employees | Average Unit Sales Price | Average Unit Cost Components | | | | Mark Up | Number of Units Sold | Total Sales Revenue | Taxes | Net Profit on Sales |
				Bargaining Unit	Other Personnel	Materials and Supplies	Allo-cated Overhead					
1983	445	130	$19.60	$ 9.185	$4.601	$1.945	$1.952	$1.917	735,850	$14,422,660	$331,721	$1,078,903
1985	417	120	20.50	9.264	4.722	2.103	2.006	2.405	718,280	14,724,740	338,669	1,388,794
1986	425	115	21.45	9.972	4.804	2.112	2.042	2.520	726,010	15,572,914	358,173	1,471,372
1987	420	110	21.98	10.263	4.812	2.163	2.092	2.650	729,530	16,035,069	369,930	1,563,325

EXHIBIT 7   Wage and Benefit Comparison—Junction Falls Area, 1987

Name of Company	Employees	Wage Rate			Average Benefits*	Holi-days	Years of Service for Vacation				
		Minimum	Maximum	Weighted Average			1 Week	2 Weeks	3 Weeks	4 Weeks	
Transgeneral Corp.	3,800	$9.50	$13.25	$10.75	$2.15	12	1/2	1	5	15	
Weary Grinders	1,200	9.10	11.80	9.90	1.06	8	–	1	10	15	
Kraft Stamping	1,410	9.30	12.80	10.55	2.27	10	1/2	1	5	15	
Woodweave, Inc.	450	9.40	11.70	9.95	1.70	8	1	5	10	20	
Hankai China Co.	640	9.05	12.15	10.05	1.95	8	1	5	15	20	
Dowel & Dovetail Co.	380	9.05	12.35	10.20	2.20	10	1/2	1	5	15	
Primo Plastic, Inc.	530	9.00	11.85	9.95	3.87	8	1	3	15	–	
Vann Fiber Co.	1,650	8.90	10.95	9.60	1.32	8	1	2	5	10	
Best Canning Co.	2,200	9.45	12.85	10.60	1.76	11	–	1	7	14	
Jinks Electric	320	9.00	11.48	9.85	1.93	9	1	5	10	20	

*Computed on weighted average wage rate, includes health and welfare, pension, and statutory benefits.

EXHIBIT 8 Wage and Benefit Comparison—Junction Falls Area, 1986

Name of Company	Employees	Wage Rate			Average Benefits*	Holi-days	Years of Service for Vacation			
		Minimum	Maximum	Weighted Average			1 Week	2 Weeks	3 Weeks	4 Weeks
Transgeneral Corp.	3,750	$8.60	12.23	$ 9.85	$1.71	11	1	5	10	15
Weary Grinders	1,200	8.30	11.00	9.06	.94	8	–	1	10	20
Kraft Stamping	1,440	8.50	12.00	9.75	2.01	9	1	3	10	15
Woodweave, Inc.	440	8.60	10.90	9.12	1.22	8	1	5	10	20
Hankai China Co.	650	8.25	11.35	9.25	1.77	8	1	5	15	20
Dowel & Dovetail Co.	372	8.25	11.55	9.40	1.98	10	1/2	1	5	15
Primo Plastic, Inc.	535	8.69	11.09	9.61	3.64	8	1	3	15	–
Vann Fiber Co.	1,700	8.10	10.15	8.80	1.04	8	1	2	5	10
Best Canning Co.	2,175	8.25	11.75	9.50	1.51	10	–	2	10	20
Jinks Electric	314	8.20	10.70	9.01	1.42	8	1	5	10	20

*Computed on weighted average wage rate, includes health and welfare, pension, and statutory benefits.

EXHIBIT 9 Wage and Benefit Comparison—Plastics Industry, Major Competitors (weighted averages—1987)

| | | Wage Rate | | | | | | | Benefits | | | | | |
| | | | | | | | | | | | Years of Service for Vacation | | | |
Name of Company	Location	Set-up	Press Oper.	Fin-isher	Genl. Shop	Slitter	Maint. Mech.	Custo-dian	Avg. Benefits	Holi-days	1 Week	2 Weeks	3 Weeks	4 Weeks
Primo Plastic, Inc.	IL	$11.48	$10.24	$ 9.90	$ 9.75	$10.10	$10.85	$ 9.00	38%	8	1	3	15	–
Wheaton, Inc.	OH	11.80	10.20	9.90	9.80	10.20	10.85	9.15	34	10	–	1	5	15
VanKleeg Precision	PA	11.60	10.20	10.05	9.80	10.15	10.78	8.85	39	8	–	1	5	25
DeLuxe Packages, Inc.	WV	11.84	10.30	10.10	9.85	10.20	10.85	9.10	27	9	–	1	10	20
Brothers Design	NC	11.50	10.20	10.00	9.80	10.10	11.00	8.90	22	8	1	2	10	20
Pearson & Kessler	NJ	11.90	10.40	10.15	9.96	10.47	10.90	9.15	31	11	1	2	10	20
TKU Mold & Label	MI	12.50	11.20	11.20	10.90	11.30	11.95	10.05	39	8	1/2	1	5	10
P3 Injection	OH	12.45	11.30	11.75	10.70	11.18	12.80	10.05	36	8	1/2	1	10	20
Continental Plastics	IN	13.00	11.40	11.20	10.95	11.50	12.05	10.25	34	10	1/2	1	10	20

EXHIBIT 10 Wage and Benefit Comparison—Plastics Industry, Major Competitors (weighted averages—1986)

| Name of Company | State | Wage Rate | | | | | | | Avg. Benefits | Holi-days | Benefits | | | |
| | | Set-up | Press Oper. | Fin-isher | Genl. Shop | Slitter | Maint. Mech. | Custo-dian | | | Years of Service for Vacation | | | |
											1 Week	2 Weeks	3 Weeks	4 Weeks
Primo Plastic, Inc.	IL	$10.46	9.33	$9.08	$8.87	$9.21	$9.89	$8.20	38%	8	1	3	15	—
Wheaton, Inc.	OH	11.10	9.54	9.33	9.10	9.50	10.15	8.55	31	10	—	1	10	20
VanKleeg Precision	PA	10.90	9.50	9.30	9.10	9.42	10.08	8.55	39	8	—	1	5	25
DeLuxe Packages, Inc.	WV	11.10	9.60	9.38	9.12	9.51	10.28	8.65	24	8	—	1	10	20
Brothers Design	NC	10.80	9.54	9.30	9.10	9.40	10.20	8.65	18	8	1	3	10	20
Pearson & Kessler	NJ	11.20	9.70	9.40	9.26	9.76	10.20	8.45	31	10	1	5	10	20
TKU Mold & Label	MI	11.80	10.54	10.44	10.21	10.60	11.25	9.40	39	8	1	5	10	20
P3 Injection	OH	11.75	10.60	10.05	10.05	10.48	11.10	9.45	34	8	1/2	1	10	20
Continental Plastics	IN	12.30	10.70	10.50	10.50	10.80	11.35	9.50	34	9	1/2	5	10	20

EXHIBIT 11 Contract Costing Assumptions

A. Health and welfare benefits.
  1. Group Life.
    $ 0.45 per $1,000 coverage in year 1.
    $ 0.47 per $1,000 coverage in year 2.
    $ 0.49 per $1,000 coverage in year 3.
    b. Each month change in service requirement changes
      cost per $1,000 coverage by $ 0.05.
  2. Sickness and accident.
    a. $ 9.00 per $1,000 coverage in year 1.
      $ 9.25 per $1,000 coverage in year 2.
      $ 9.50 per $1,000 coverage in year 3.
    b. Each month change in service requirement changes
      cost per $1,000 coverage by $ 0.05.
    c. Every one-week change in "maximum weeks" coverage
      changes cost per $1,000 coverage by $ 0.35.
  3. Long-term disability.
    a. $ 4.50 per $1,000 coverage in year 1.
      $ 4.65 per $1,000 coverage in year 2.
      $ 4.80 per $1,000 coverage in year 3.
    b. Each month change in service requirement changes
      cost per $1,000 coverage by $ 0.05.
    c. Every one-week change in qualifying period changes
      cost per $1,000 coverage by $ 0.06.
  4. Comprehensive medical.
    a. Individual Coverage.
      $ 330 per year per worker in year 1.
      $ 345 per year per worker in year 2.
      $ 355 per year per worker in year 3.
    b. Family Coverage.
      $ 700 per year per worker in year 1.
      $ 740 per year per worker in year 2.
      $ 760 per year per worker in year 3.
    c. 65 percent of employees are provided family coverage.
    d. Every 1 percent reduction in cost coverage due to cost sharing reduces
      costs by 1 percent.
    e. Every 1 percent reduction in company's percent premium paid reduces
      cost of coverage by 1 percent.
    f. Each month reduction in eligibility requirement reduces employer's cost
      of coverage by $10.
    g. Every $1 change in deductible changes cost of coverage by $ 0.80.
    h. Every $1,000 change in maximum annual premium paid changes cost
      by $7.50 annually; every $1,000 change in maximum for dependent
      changes cost of coverage by $7.00.
    i. Every $1,000 change in maximum lifetime premium paid changes cost
      by $1.00 for individual and $1.50 for dependents.

EXHIBIT 11—*Concluded*

B. Pensions.
  1. General.
    a. Every .1 percent point change in "Percent of annual wage (last 5 years)" changes pension costs by .05 percent.
    b. Every one-year change in retirement changes costs by .25 percent.
  2. ERISA-approved vesting options (through 12/31/88).
    a. Cliff (after 10 years)   = 11.0 percent of annual wage.
    b. Graded (50 percent after 5 years) = 13.0 percent of annual wage.
    c. Graded (25 percent after 5 years) = 12.0 percent of annual wage.
    d. Rule of 45   = 9.5 percent of annual wage.
  3. ERISA-approved vesting options (after 12/31/88).
    a. Cliff (after 5 years)   = 16.0 percent of annual wage.
    b. Graded (20 percent after 3 years;
       20 percent annually thereafter) = 17.0 percent of annual wage.
C. Overtime.
  If distribution of overtime is changed, overtime costs increase as follows:
    Even distribution = 5 percent.
    Seniority by job   = 7 percent.
    Seniority by plant = 10 percent.

Appendix

AGREEMENT

Between

PRIMO PLASTIC, INC.
JUNCTION FALLS, ILLINOIS

and the

ASSOCIATED RUBBER AND PLASTICS SPECIALTY WORKERS
LOCAL UNION NO. 488

This Agreement made and entered into this 19th day of December 1985, between Primo Plastic, Inc.—Junction Falls Plant, hereinafter designated as the "Company" and the Associated Rubber and Plastics Specialty Workers—Local 488, hereinafter designated as the "Union."

WITNESSETH:

Article I
Definitions

Section 1. Where the words are used in this Agreement, "Company" means the Primo Plastic, Inc. plant located in Junction Falls, Illinois; "Union" means the Associated Rubber and Plastics Specialty Workers, Local 488; and "Employee" means all production and maintenance employees and those associated with production and maintenance, including setup operators, maintenance mechanics, press operators, slitters, finishers, general shop workers and custodians.

Article II
Union Recognition

Section 1. The Union hereby represents to the Company that its officers and representatives who sign this Agreement in its name have been granted the authority to make this agreement in behalf of the Union.

Section 2. The principles and determinations set forth in the provisions of this Agreement will be carried out with the expectation that the matter of employees and Company relationship will be maintained on a harmonious and sensible basis.

Section 3. The Union is hereby recognized as the sole and exclusive bargaining agent.

Article III
Union Membership Requirements
and Check-Off

Section 1. The Labor-Management Relations Act, 1947, as amended, having been complied with, the parties agree as follows:

1. It is agreed subject to the provisions of the Labor-Management Relations Act of 1947, as amended, that all employees in the bargaining unit shall, after the thirtieth (30th) day of employment or thirty (30) days following the date of this Agreement, whichever is later, as a condition of employment, become and remain members of the Union and shall keep themselves in good standing for the duration of this Agreement subject, however, to the following conditions and exceptions:

A. The Company shall have the right to choose any person as a new employee. Every new employee shall be a temporary employee for a period of sixty (60) days from the date s/he first reports for work.

B. The Union shall accept without discrimination, the membership application of any new employee who applies in accordance with the thirty (30) day requirement set forth in SECTION 1 above, and it shall not refuse membership to such employee except for good and sufficient reason.

Section 2. The Company will deduct, for the period of this Agreement, from the wages payable to any eligible employee or Union member who shall have given the Company a written order to do so, such amount of Union dues or uniform local initiation fee as shall be owing by such member. All dues so deducted will be forwarded to the Office of the National Secretary-Treasurer or other National officer of the Union duly designated in writing to receive the same and to the Financial Secretary of the Local in such proportion as designated by the National Secretary-Treasurer.

Article IV
Responsibilities of Union
and Company

Section 1. During the term of this Agreement the Union agrees that there shall be no strikes, slowdowns, work stoppages, or interruption or impeding of work.

The company will not lock out any employee represented by the Union.

Section 2. The Company is responsible, as the Union recognizes, for the management and operation of the plant and for the efficiency, direction, order, and discipline of the working forces; and it is agreed that the Company may hire, promote, demote, transfer, drop or lay-off for lack of business and suspend or discharge employees for proper causes; and that the right to do so is vested exclusively in the Company; provided that no action so taken shall be in violation of any other provision of this Agreement and that the Company shall not use this right for the purpose of discrimination against any employee because of his/her membership or legitimate activity in the Union.

Article V
Seniority

Section 1. In the event of increase or decrease of personnel due to changes in methods of operation or business conditions, length of continuous service shall prevail as between employees physically fit and competent through knowledge, training, skill and efficiency to perform the available work.

Section 2. Senior employees shall be given a reasonable opportunity to prove their competency.

Section 3. Should the Union consider the Company's decision on any question of competency unreasonable, it shall become a matter for consideration as a grievance by the representatives of the Union and the Company in the manner provided in this Agreement.

Section 4. In the event of any vacancy or promotion (except in positions where technical training, special experience, or special education is required) length of continuous service shall prevail as between employees physically fit and competent through the available work.

Section 5. Continuous service or seniority is determined by the length of service computed in years, months and days from the last date of the beginning of an employee's employment by the Company.

Section 6. An employee wishing to transfer from one department to another may make application to the Central Employment Office. The Company shall place the application on file in accordance with the applicant's seniority. When an employee accepts a transfer all other transfers they have on file are discarded. The Company may fill nonclassified jobs on a temporary basis for up to forty-five (45) days.

Section 7. When an employee is transferred from one department to another, at the request of the Company, on a temporary basis, the employees affected shall be so notified and the action recorded; and when the former job is back in operation such employees shall have preference.

Article VI
Absence

Regular attendance is expected of every employee. Absence reports should be made orally by telephone or otherwise to the Personnel Department and should be confirmed in writing within five (5) days for the protection of the worker and to avoid misunderstandings between employees and Company. Seven (7) consecutive working days absence without written report constitutes cause for removal from rolls, with any subsequent reemployment being without credit for previous service. Failure to report to the Company within seven (7) consecutive days after the expiration of a leave of absence, or other periods of absence of specified duration, constitutes cause for removal from rolls, with any subsequent reemployment being without credit for previous service.

Article VII
Workweek, Holidays, and
Premium Pay

Section 1. A regular workweek consisting of seven (7) consecutive days shall be established by the Company for each department or group of employees. Such workweek shall start and end at the same time each week. Each day in the workweek will be considered a scheduled day. A workday shall consist of twenty-four (24) consecutive hours from the time an employee starts work.

Section 2. Eight (8) holidays, as listed below, will be designated as recognized holidays:

New Year's
Washington's Birthday
Memorial Day
Fourth of July
Labor Day
Veterans' Day
Thanksgiving Day
Christmas Day

Section 3. Premium rates are to be computed on the basis of average hourly earnings, for the workweek or the workday in which the premium applies.

A. Time worked in excess of eight (8) hours in one (1) workday will be paid at time and one-half rate.

B. Time worked on the calendar day Sunday will be paid at time and one-half rate.

C. Time worked in excess of forty (40) hours in any workweek for which time and one-half has not been paid under rules A or B will be paid at time and one-half rate.

D. Holiday overtime cannot be permitted when such time coincides with other overtime. When a designated holiday falls on Sunday, the beginning of the holiday will be delayed twenty-four (24) hours. Further, if any of these designated holidays are declared by Federal law to be celebrated on Monday, then the said designated holiday shall be celebrated on such Monday.

E. The employee must work on both his/her last regularly scheduled workday immediately preceding the holiday and on his/her first regularly scheduled workday following the holiday.

Article VIII
Work Outside Normal Schedule

Section 1. Employees are not to start work before their regular scheduled starting time.

Section 2. If an employee is requested by a supervisor to report for work before his/her regular scheduled starting time in order to make special preparations s/he will be paid according to rules governing pay under the terms of this Agreement.

Article IX
Temporary Work Assignments

Section 1. An employee temporarily assigned to a job paying a lower rate at the request of the Company will be paid his/her regular rate if the employee is fully qualified to perform his/her former work assignment and if the regular job is available.

Section 2. Such temporary assignment of an employee to a lower-rated hourly job at the pay rate on the higher-rated job will not constitute a change in rate of pay for the lower hourly rated job.

Section 3. Nothing in the foregoing shall affect the practice of employees voluntarily working overtime on temporary work assignments outside their regular work schedules as relief during manpower shortages.

Article X
Call-In Pay

Section 1. The Company agrees not to call employees to work when no work is available, and agrees to plan so that an employee finishing one (1) day may know whether or not to report the next day.

Section 2. The Company will make reasonable effort to notify employees when not to report for work. If an employee has been regularly scheduled or notified to report for work and is not thereafter given reasonable notice by the supervisor that work is not available, and reports for work, the Company will guarantee four (4) hours of work, or four (4) hours of pay at the employee's base rate for his/her scheduled work, except in cases where the lack of available work is caused by conditions over which management has no control.

Article XI
Division of Overtime

The Company will endeavor to divide overtime equally among qualified employees within reasonable periods of time, provided that such division does not interfere with efficient operations in the department.

Article XII
Working Conditions and Methods

Section 1. The management's policy of expansion of output and cost reduction through mechanical improvement, plant rearrangement, or additions and developments is of vital importance to employees and Company. The elements of methods, speeds, equipment, etc., are the exclusive responsibility of management for the production and sale of material of good quality, produced at a cost free of disadvantages in a competitive market. There shall be no limit on or curtailment of production.

Section 2. The Company states that it is not its intention to change any of the working conditions now in effect in its plants and not covered by this Agreement for the purpose of discriminating against the Union or its members, and that no such change will be made except for the purpose of improving the production or the efficiency of the plan.

Section 3. This does not deny the workers the right to confer with management in regard to speeds, setup, temperatures and working conditions.

Section 4. Where for better and more efficient operation it is deemed necessary to establish new shift operations, such shifts will be established and classified by the Company as rotating, or nonrotating shifts.

Section 5. When an employee is not satisfactorily performing his/her work s/he shall be so notified by his/her supervisor and s/he shall also be notified before notations regarding such work are put on his/her R-29. If an employee requests it, his/her R-29 will be available for his/her inspection.

Article XIII
Factory Rules

Section 1. The Company shall have the right to make and, after proper publication thereof, to enforce any reasonable factory rule. Should the Union consider any such rule unreasonable, it shall be a matter for joint consideration as a grievance by the representatives of the Union and those of the Company, under this Agreement. It is recognized that factory rules, forbidding the following offenses, are at present in force, and that any violation thereof by an employee shall justify the Company in imposing the penalty of suspension or discharge:

A. Insubordination, inefficiency or incompetency of any employee.

B. Failure to conform to rules of the Company, public laws, or regulations pertaining to health or safety.

C. Bringing intoxicating liquors into the plant, use of intoxicating liquors on Company property, or reporting for work or working while under the influence of liquor. (Also applies to narcotics in any form.)

D. Willful destruction, damage, or stealing of any Company property or the property of any employee on Company premises.

E. Fighting, using abusive language, or gambling on Company property.

F. Careless or willful contamination of batch.

G. Purchasing the favor of supervisor by giving or loaning money or making gifts, etc. Both the employee and supervisor shall suffer a like penalty.

H. Altering time punched in or out on time card, or punching another employee's time card.

I. Smoking in prohibited areas.

J. Willful hindering or limiting production.

K. Sleeping during working hours.

L. Habitual carelessness or recklessness, playing of tricks or pranks dangerous to other employees.

M. Any employee subject to discharge for infraction of any such Company rule, shall have the right to a hearing if s/he desires it; and the case of any employee desiring such hearing shall be handled as a grievance under this Agreement.

Article XIV
Vacation Plan

Section 1. The vacation plan for employees on the hourly payroll is designated, to afford an employee relaxation that will prepare him for work during the coming year.

Section 2. Employees with one (1) or more years of continuous service on July 1 of the vacation year will qualify for one (1) week of vacation. Employees with three (3) or more years of continuous service on July 1 of the vacation year will qualify for two (2) weeks vacation. Employees with fifteen (15) or more years of continuous service on July 1 of the vacation year will qualify for three (3) weeks vacation.

Section 3. Any vacation not completed during a calendar year cannot be carried over to the next year. Vacation will, so far as possible be granted at times most desired by employees, but the final right to allotment of vacation period is reserved by the Company so that orderly operations of the plant may be insured.

Section 4. If, in the opinion of the Company, the vacation plan interferes with the attainment of maximum production, an eligible employee may be required to continue work and receive vacation pay in lieu of actual vacation from work. However, it is the intent that, to the greatest degree possible in the Company's judgment, eligible employees shall receive the benefit of vacation from work, and shall take such vacation. In the final analysis, whether an employee takes his/her vacation or not is up to the Company; in other words, vacations shall not be compulsory. Further, the Company reserves the right to shut down any or all of its departments for part or all of the vacation periods and to have the employees take their vacations at such times.

Article XV
Continuation of Present Privileges

Section 1. It is the intention of the Company to continue all existing benefits for the welfare of its employees not inconsistent with this Agreement insofar as is practicable, but it is understood that the benefits granted are purely voluntary on the part of the Company and may be changed by the Company in whole or in part, or completely withdrawn when in its judgment such action becomes necessary after notice to and consultation with the Union.

Article XVI
Grievance Procedure

Section 1. Any grievance or misunderstanding which any employee or employees represented by the Union may desire to discuss and adjust with the Company shall be handled as follows:

Step 1. Must be taken up between the employee and his/her immediate supervisor. This does not prohibit the employee from being accompanied by his/her Shop Committeeperson.

If no agreement is reached with the immediate Supervisor, the employee and his/her Department Executive Committeeperson then may take the grievance up with the employee's Department Supervisor.

If no agreement is reached with the Department Supervisor, the employee and his/her Department Executive Committeeperson then may take the grievance up with the employee's Personnel Supervisor/Production Superintendent.

If no agreement is reached with the Personnel Supervisor/Production Superintendent the employee and his/her Department Executive Committeeperson then may take the grievance up with the employee's Plant Manager.

Step 2. If no agreement is reached with the Plant Manager, the employee, his/her Department Executive Committeeperson, and the Local Union President then may take the grievance up with the Company's Director of Labor Relations.

Step 3. A grievance not satisfactorily settled in Step 2 may be referred to the Local Union Executive Committee. If the Executive Committee feels that the grievance is justified, the Local Union will notify the National Union that it wishes to process the grievance to Step 3. A grievance meeting then will be scheduled between the employee, his/her Department Executive Committeeperson, the Local Union President, and the National Union President or his/her designee.

Step 4. If the grievance is not settled in Step 3, it may be submitted to arbitration at the request of either the National President of the union or the Vice President and Director of Industrial Relations, and the decision of the arbitrator will be final and binding. Notice of the request to arbitrate the grievance must be served on the other party within thirty (30) days after the termination of proceedings in Step 3 unless extended by mutual agreement. Thereafter, and as soon as possible, the National President of the Union or the Vice President and Director of Industrial Relations, or both, or their designated representatives, shall request Federal Mediation and Conciliation Service to submit to each a panel of seven (7) arbitrators from which panel the parties shall alternately strike one (1) name from the panel until one (1) remains who shall be the arbitrator to hear and decide the dispute. The right to strike the first name shall be determined by a toss of a coin.

The arbitrator so selected shall have no power to add to, subtract from, or modify any of the provisions of this contract. Each party shall pay one half of the fees and expenses of the arbitrator. The decision of the arbitrator shall be transmitted in writing to the parties within thirty (30) days after the completion of the hearing.

Article XVII
Wage Rates

Section 1. Recognizing that the welfare of its employees and their opportunities to earn a living depend upon the success and prosperity of the Company and further recognizing that the various wages provided for in this Agreement are of a substantial nature, the Union hereby pledges for itself and all its members—the employees of the Company—that they will perform their work effectively and efficiently to the best of their ability, and will cooperate in the introduction or installation of such processes, machinery, changes in or introduction of new methods of operation, incentive pay plans or systems, and job classification and evaluation plans or systems as the Company may introduce or put into effect for the purpose of better and more efficient operation to the end that the Company may increase production and reduce costs so that the Company may adequately meet competitive conditions, and maintain employment.

Section 2. Wage rates as agreed upon shall be on file at the Labor Relations office of the Company and shall remain undisturbed for the life of the Agreement, except when a change in, or introduction of new methods of operation, incentive pay, or job classification and evaluation shall require change. However, individual rates may be changed by mutual agreement, or by handling as a grievance under this Agreement.

Section 3. The Union further pledges for itself and its members that they will fully cooperate in the following: The reduction or shrinkages of all kinds; in the saving of materials, tools, machinery, equipment, and all Company property by means of careful handling and use; in minimizing breakage and losses of any kind caused by careless handling; in maintaining a high standard of quality in all products through efficient and careful workmanship; in aiding in the enforcement of all factory rules, regulations, safety and health measures; and in cooperation to the best interests of the Union and the Company.

Section 4. It is recognized by the Company and the Union that they both must use their best efforts to reduce absenteeism to a minimum. The Union agrees to take appropriate and proper measures to curb absenteeism among its members at all times.

Article XVIII
Employees Injured

Section 1. Any employee injured while on duty, and leaving work with the approval of the Company doctor, or other authorized Company representative, shall receive his/her full pay for that day's work at his/her hourly rate, regardless of the time injured.

Section 2. In the event an employee commences a new period of total disability on or after the date of this Agreement as a result of occupational injury or disease which was incurred prior to the date of this Agreement, the Company will pay a supplementary benefit. Such supplementary benefit shall not exceed twenty-six (26) weeks for each such period of total disability nor shall the supplementary benefit when combined with the Workers' Compensation benefit exceed the weekly benefit which would have been payable had the disability resulted from nonoccupational causes.

Article XIX
Supervisors

Section 1. Supervisors or salaried workers shall not perform work customarily performed by Union members, except in cases of emergency, experimental work, instruction, and the making of minor adjustments and changes.

Article XX
Pension and Insurance Program

Attached hereto and incorporated herein as Exhibit A is the Insurance Program agreed upon between the parties, the same to continue unchanged during the term of this Agreement.

Article XXI
General Provisions

1. This Agreement is in full settlement of all the issues in dispute between the Company and the Union.

2. Between November 1, 1986, and December 31, 1986, at a mutually agreeable time, a joint session of not over five (5) days will be set aside to handle such unsettled grievances, as may have accumulated, within the terms of the Agreement.

Article XXII
Cancellation of Certain
Portions of Old Agreement

Section 1. This Agreement cancels and supersedes all of the provisions of the previous Agreement between the parties hereto dated January 26, 1982, unless otherwise provided for herein.

Article XXIII
Time Off for Death in Family

Section 1. In the event of the death of the parent, brother, sister, mother-in-law, father-in-law, stepmother-in-law, stepfather-in-law, daughter-in-law, son-in-law, stepchild, stepparent, stepsister, stepbrother, half sister, half brother, grandchild or grandparent of any employee, who has been in the employ of the

Company for at least thirty (30) days, the employee shall be paid for time lost through date of interment, not in excess of three (3) shifts at base rate, provided the employee attends the funeral and furnishes proof thereof, if requested by the Company. In no event shall an employee receive more than three (3) shifts pay at base rate under this Section I.

Section 2. In the event of the death of the wife, husband, son or daughter of any employee, who has been in the employ of the Company for at least thirty (30) days, the employee shall be paid for time lost, not in excess of five (5) shifts at base rate, provided the employee attends the funeral and furnishes proof thereof, if requested by the Company. In no event shall an employee receive more than five (5) shifts pay at base rate under this Section 2.

Article XXIV
Jury Service

Section 1. In the event an employee on the active payroll is called for jury service, s/he shall be excused from work for each such day on which s/he serves or reports to serve and shall be paid for the time necessarily lost from his/her regular work schedule due to such jury service, provided s/he notifies the Company of his/her intended absence. The pay shall be the difference between each day's jury fee (exclusive of travel allowance) and the pay for hours of work necessarily lost computed at his/her individual rate for the work s/he would have performed. Such unworked hours, limited to a maximum of eight (8) hours each day, will be counted as though they were worked, for the purpose of establishing forty (40) hours worked. An employee excused from jury service shall report to work at the beginning of his/her next regularly scheduled shift. The employee will present proof of service of a jury duty notice or summons and the amount of pay received for such jury service.

Article XXV
No Discrimination and Equal
Opportunity Employer

Section 1. Both the Company and the Union agree that there will be no discrimination between employees or applicants for employment for reasons of race, creed, sex, color, age, national origin, marital status or nonjob related disability and to comply with State and Federal laws pertaining thereto.

Article XXVI
Term of Contract

Section 1. This Agreement shall become effective on the date of its execution and thereafter shall continue in force from year to year, unless either party hereto shall notify the other in writing at least ninety (90) days prior to the end of the current term, or as the case may be, ninety (90) days prior to the end of any additional contract year, of an intention to make changes in or terminate this Agreement. Such written notice shall specify any changes or amendments desired by the party giving such notice and shall be sent by registered mail.

Exhibit A
Insurance Programs

Section 1. The Company shall administer a comprehensive group life, sickness and accident, long-term disability, and major medical insurance program covering employees who comply with the eligibility and qualification requirements.

Section 2. This Program shall be extended as described herein. Future increases in the cost of the Program will be paid for by the Company.

Section 3. The Program shall include the following:

(a) Group life insurance equal to 1.5 times the employee's annual base wage after one month of credited service.

(b) Weekly sickness and accident benefits for employees with one month of credited service for nonwork-connected disabilities up to 26 weeks duration. Amount of benefit will be equal to 65 percent of an employee's annual base earnings.

(c) Long-term disability (LTD) benefits for employees with two months of credited service and after 26 weeks of disability. LTD benefits will equal 60 percent of the disabled employee's annual base earnings.

(d) Comprehensive major medical insurance for both employees (with one month credited service) and covered dependents, with a $100 deductible for employee coverage and a $200 deductible for coverage of each dependent; with 20 percent coinsurance for reasonable and customary charges. The maximum annual charges are $10,000 per covered employee and $5,000 per covered dependent. Maximum lifetime charges are $250,000 per employee and $100,000 per covered dependent.

Exhibit B
Pension Agreement

Section 1. Retirement benefits now being paid under the Consolidated Service Retirement Plan shall be continued without change for all employees who retired under the terms of the Plan.

Section 2. The retirement benefits of the Consolidated Service Retirement Plan shall be continued for those employees retiring on and after December 19, 1982 as follows:

The normal annual pension benefit shall be calculated by multiplying two (2) amounts:

(1) The number of years and months of Credited Service up to age 70 of the employee and date of retirement, and (2) 1.5 percent of the employee's last five years' average annual W-2 earnings.

Section 3. The Company is exclusively responsible for maintaining an ERISA-qualified plan with no contribution from employees. In the event Federal or State law amends provisions under ERISA that effect employee qualification or cost of this Pension Agreement, the Company and Union will meet and negotiate in good faith over any revisions to this Agreement. The Union will have the right to strike in the event that the parties cannot come to agreement over modifications to the Plan.

Section 4. Employees become eligible for receipt of benefits and benefits are fully vested after an employee has earned ten (10) years of credited service.

Section 5. Employees receive full benefits under the Plan upon retirement at age 65 or later.

An employee age 55 or older with 10 years or more of credited service who retires may elect to receive actuarially reduced benefits under the Plan.

Section 6. An employee with 10 or more years of credited service who has been permanently and totally disabled for six months may retire with a monthly pension benefit calculated on credited service to his/her retirement date without any actuarial reduction.

Cynex and the United Brotherhood of Production Workers

Gene Michaels, plant manager of the Cynex facility of Darbough-Jones, stared out his office window at the lights gleaming off of car windshields in the plant parking lot. The contract with the United Brotherhood of Production Workers Local 819 had expired at midnight the day before, but the negotiation teams had granted a 24-hour extension. Once the extension had been granted, Michaels became formally involved in negotiations. The teams were to meet again in half an hour. This was Michaels' fifth round of negotiations with Local 819, but it seemed that each round was tougher than the last. In 1981, a two-year wage freeze was negotiated during a time of continued layoffs. By the 1984 negotiations, layoffs had ceased and corporate directed Michaels to negotiate an employee involvement program (EIP) in conjunction with a newly adopted participative management style. Local 819's president, Landers Dion, saw employee involvement as a threat to union prerogatives and worker job security despite support for EIP from the union's regional office. Local 819 went out on strike when the contract expired on April 10, 1984. They returned 33 days later, after Cynex agreed to a "Best Effort to Transfer" (BET) layoff provision in the contract, which included a 60-day notice of potential displacements.

By 1987 the union was touting the three years of the EIP as an unequivocal success: cost reductions within the Reman work unit of 8 percent, 18 percent, and 14 percent were realized in the first, second, and third years of the program, respectively. Other subsequently involved units were realizing similar gains. Many of the gains were in reducing the time it took to get prototypes from New Products into production. This greatly reduced lead time, which in turn increased customer orders. As a result, workers displaced as a result of recommendations were transferred to other lines as customer demand continued to grow.

Dion was urging expansion of EIP into all work units, including the five units of the new products area, and implementation of a gainsharing plan. Under Cynex's supplier development program (SDP), New Products worked closely with single-sourced outside suppliers in the development and production of prototypes of all new products introduced since 1983. Not only had SDP greatly reduced Cynex's prototype development time and costs, management also believed that it reduced direct labor costs in new product production.

In addition to pressure from Dion on expanding EIP, Michaels was being pressured by Darbough-Jones's Finance Department to negotiate concessions that would reduce labor costs by 15–20 percent. To obtain these savings, corporate wanted Cynex to reduce job classifications by 20 percent; specifically, corporate suggested that Cynex function with just one maintenance department (versus the current two-department classification) and urged that labor grades for numerically controlled (N/C) and computer-controlled (C) production machinery be made equal given recent retrofitting of computer controls on N/C machines. Moreover, corporate felt that some flexibility with seniority contract provisions would be necessary to maintain competitiveness.

Michaels glanced at his watch: 9:55 P.M. Dion, he knew, would be late.

COMPANY HISTORY

In 1986, Darbough-Jones reported annual sales of over $150 million from their two main operating divisions: Financial Services and Operating Systems (see Exhibit 1, p. 70). Henry Darbough had started Darbough Machine Parts in 1911 with a patent on a lathe cog that increased cutting accuracy to .002 of an inch. Darbough, a known tinkerer, steadily expanded and improved his assortment of tooling parts and instigated an intensive R&D department within the company in 1928. His foresight allowed Darbough Machine Parts to continue operations through the depression by remaining the sole solvent source for their niche of small-to medium-sized durable goods manufacturers.

In 1935, Darbough joined with Jones Assembly Systems, a designer and supplier to companies utilizing the assembly-line manufacturing technique. The newly formed Darbough-Jones continued to stress R&D for ingenious tooling components; Jones brought in the philosophy of customer service. In 1959, Darbough-Jones purchased ACF Financial Management, making it an adjunct to the customer service department by enabling the company to arrange attractive leasing or lending options for potential customers. By the mid-70s, the ACF office was involved in financial services to noncustomers as well. Revenues from ACF continued to be an increasing proportion of aftertax profit, so that in 1981, Darbough-Jones reorganized to allow ACF to function as a separate operating division, Financial Services, with numerous branch offices throughout North America, and an international office in Brussels (see Exhibit 2 for Darbough-Jones' current organization, p. 71).

During the 60s, Darbough-Jones purchased three domestic machining-related plants. Stuart Darbough, Henry Darbough's son, however, believed the company's traditional market was changing. Darbough-Jones's commitment to stay preeminent in technology resulted in the 1964 purchase of Cynex Limited, a small, privately owned manufacturer of transistors located in southern Illinois, and the 1965 purchase of Goettner G.m.b.H., a small German electronics firm.

The company perceived the benefits of "cross pollinating" German and domestic electrical engineers and implemented the Strategic Learning Program. From 1965 through 1968, members of each engineering staff were required to undergo a six-month internship at the sister facility. Internships at the German facility were research oriented. Capital investment to integrate the electronic technology with traditional machine-tool technology occurred only at the Cynex plant, and internships there stressed collaboration with mechanical engineers to apply research to machine tools. Bonuses and promotion for the engineering staff were predicated on the successful production of prototypes. The Strategic Learning Program was evaluated positively when Darbough-Jones won three out of five New Product awards for their Electrically-Controlled Blue Punch introduced at the 1968 Annual Tooling and Manufacturing Systems Conference and orders from the Conference were shipped within six months.

As integrated circuit (IC) technology evolved, however, Darbough-Jones phased out transistor production and decided not to compete in IC chip production with the large domestic and offshore manufacturers. Instead, the technology was outsourced from numerous suppliers and integrated by applications engineers at the Cynex facility. Goettner was subsequently sold in 1980.

Using multiple suppliers became a nightmare for Cynex. Offshore and domestic suppliers used different specifications for identical products, resulting in duplication of inventory. Moreover, lead times from offshore suppliers, normally awarded a bid on the basis of price, were causing delays in new-product introduction. As lead times extended, Cynex customers canceled orders.

In 1981, Darbough-Jones instigated the Supplier Development Program, offering fewer suppliers longer contracts in exchange for technical assistance in the design of new products. While new-product engineering, machining, and assembly still resided within the Cynex facility, ongoing relations with outside component suppliers were maintained within the purchasing department at the St. Louis corporate office 70 miles away.

THE CYNEX PLANT

The Cynex facility produced both traditional and experimental machine tooling subassemblies for systems designed by their engineering/sales staff and their customers. While their customers' systems were unique, Cynex developed tooling subassemblies that could be utilized in a variety of production systems, and therefore mass-produced.

Gene Michaels had been with Darbough-Jones since 1967, starting as a production operations management trainee following his graduation from Ohio State's Department of Mechanical Engineering. In September 1974, he was promoted to assistant plant manager at Cynex. Having demonstrated his ability to handle labor relations effectively, he also was given considerable responsibility in contract negotiations with the union in 1975. Cynex labor-management relations became increasingly important to corporate as cost pressures increased within the tooling market. Dave Peters, Corporate Director of Labor Relations at Darbough-Jones, granted Michaels wide discretion in informally directing local negotiations at the Cynex facility after Michaels's promotion to plant manager in 1977.

Michaels had been instrumental in implementing the Supplier Development Program, which he felt would enable Cynex to win back customers lost due to production delays. He had heatedly objected, however, to corporate's decision to maintain supplier relationships within purchasing at corporate headquarters. His contact with the suppliers was largely limited to their field service representatives, most of whom had engineering backgrounds like himself.

During implementation of the Supplier Development Program, Cynex production was divided into two areas: Machining Systems and New Products (see Exhibit 3, p. 72). Prototype development for any new product remained within the five production departments under New Products. Once a production prototype was accepted by both design engineers and expeditors, production shifted into the six departments under Machining Systems. Maintenance was provided to each area by two maintenance departments: electrical and mechanical.

Generally, labor grades were higher within New Products, as all work was custom-built until it passed into Machining Systems, where production was either numerically controlled or computer controlled (see Exhibits 4 and 5, pp. 73 and 75, for job classifications and wage rates). Because of the skill level required, the most senior union members generally were employed within New Products. New Products production employees worked with the design engineers and technical staff in the execution of prototypes but had little input into production design decisions. There was no interface between New Products and Machining Systems. Production scheduling of prototypes was simply made by the general foreman.

It had been at Michaels' request that Cynex was divided into the two work areas (New Products and Machining Systems) following full implementation of the Supplier Development Program. Dion had expressed concern with the decision, however, fearing a de facto split within the union membership.

LOCAL 819

Before the 1964 purchase by Darbough-Jones, Cynex Ltd.'s dominant labor union for the 240 hourly employees (85 percent female) was the International Union of Electrical Workers. Within two years, however, Darbough-Jones expended over $7 million to upgrade and integrate the facility with traditional tooling operations. Over this two-year period, 780 additional production workers were hired from three surrounding communities. While workers continued to enjoy wages and benefits slightly better than local industry, supervisor-worker relations worsened, sometimes becoming bitter. This problem seemed to arise because original Cynex Ltd. supervisors were transferred into tooling operations; workers felt that these supervisors had little knowledge of tooling operations, and management all but ignored shop-floor problems between supervisors and the rank and file. Moreover, the sales staff put considerable pressure on the general foreman to meet promised delivery dates. When this failed to produce results, some of the sales people would take their requests directly to the shop floor, where some supervisors would schedule overtime shifts as a special favor.

By 1969, the promise of a grievance procedure and greater control over scheduling, especially overtime, was a strong draw for union representation. In the summer of 1970, Local 819 of the United Brotherhood of Production Workers easily won recognition as the bargaining representative of all production maintenance and skilled workers at Cynex. First contract negotiations not only resulted in a grievance procedure and greater control over scheduling of work, but also a seniority system, and an upgrade in the job classifications of 52 semiskilled workers. Workers overwhelmingly elected Landers Dion union president.

Dion was one of the first workers hired after the plant purchase. He had previously worked as a machinist in a local automotive rebuild shop. His fumbling, Columbo-like manner belied his cleverness and his ability to maneuver around Michaels. But Michaels liked Dion, who took his obligation to the workers very seriously. As Dion often put it, "Hell, these just ain't union members, they're my neighbors!" The loyalty this attitude inspired among the workers was instrumental in their voting to go out on strike in 1984.

Dion was generally highly regarded by elected officials at both the regional and national union offices and recently had been appointed to the UBPW National Committee on Quality of Work Life. Dion attended all regional and national conventions, where he maintained high visibility with his outspoken support of employees' rights to a share of company profits. There was some discussion that this issue would become a platform for him in the upcoming national elections.

COLLECTIVE BARGAINING HISTORY

The 1972 negotiations resulted in extending the contract period to three years, a 6 percent wage increase, and the implementation of a cost of living allowance (COLA).

The 1975 contract resulted in a modest wage increase, but maintenance of the COLA. Shortly after the contract went into effect, sales growth for Cynex flattened. Local 819's COLA provision cut alarmingly into gross margin. To compensate, Cynex brought in the new supplier-technology of integrated circuitry more quickly than originally planned, phasing out transistor production. Consequently, 139 hourly employees within Electrical Sub-Assembly were laid off by mid-1976. Not surprisingly, the number of grievances initiated by Local 819 members nearly doubled, and product quality declined.

During 1978 negotiations, management vigorously contended that their market had not yet returned despite slight improvement in sales over the past year. While products containing integrated circuit technology were creating an initial increase in sales, supplier problems and late deliveries were resulting in cancellations. Moreover, inflation escalated costs, only part of which could be passed on to the customers that didn't cancel. Cynex bargained to put a ceiling on yearly COLAs. The union conceded.

1981 negotiations came at a time of the worst sales performance in Cynex's history. Corporate cut back on R&D while implementing the Supplier Development Program, anticipating that the chosen suppliers would pick up part of the product development cost. Corporate further demanded dramatic cost-savings in production of current product lines. As a result, 10 percent of New Products employees were technically laid off; portions of Reman were subcontracted out, resulting in a 5 percent reduction in Machining Systems' work force; and Michaels' negotiation team bargained hard for a wage freeze and abolishment of the COLA.

Because of seniority provisions in the contract, the displaced New Products employees were allowed to bump less senior union members within Machining Systems. As a result, jobs requiring semiskilled workers were being filled by skilled workers, at a wage rate equivalent to their previous job. Since these skilled workers were not familiar with the production technology within Machining Systems, scrappage and rework rates increased, and product quality decreased. Conflicts between these skilled workers and supervisors resulted in a substantial increase in the number of grievances filed and unexcused absences. While Dion realized that concessions within this labor-management climate would fan the fires, Michaels also made it clear that without them, layoffs would escalate. The union conceded the wage freeze; management backed off on its COLA demand.

By late 1982, corporate announced its intentions of allocating a larger portion of sales to R&D during 1983. As a result, some of the skilled workers were reassigned to New Products, and Machining Systems rehired some of the laid-off employees. Darbough-Jones, however, was reorganizing in response to the CEO's directive to "be more competitive in the face of dynamic market conditions by utilizing all of our differential assets to their fullest." As stated in the 1983 annual report, part of this vision entailed a participative management strategy, the Interactive Human Resource (IHR) program, aimed at "gaining valuable input from all members of the organization in an effort to satisfy the divergent needs of all our employees by combining our knowledge to keep Darbough-Jones competitive and profitable."

As a result, Darbough-Jones had instigated an employee involvement program at their nonunion DataSync facility the year following an unsuccessful union organizing drive. While corporate maintained that this was merely part of the new management strategy, local union supporters viewed the program as an attempt to undermine union support.

When Michaels approached Dion during 1984 negotiations with the concept of employee involvement, Dion flatly refused to discuss the subject.

"First of all," Dion retorted, "Anything in the annual report is a lot of hooey to make the stockholders think we're into fancy-shmansy management stuff. It'll all blow over before your PR guys write the next report."

Dion was also concerned about how the workers would react. Despite the wage concession in 1981, layoffs had continued for over a year, and the trend was just recently reversing. Dion viewed the proposed work-team concept as a threat to the job security of workers that had just been through tough times. Moreover, the split in the membership as a result of the layoffs and bumping between New Products and Machining Systems employees, as well as the subcontracting out of portions of

Reman, had left Machining Systems semiskilled workers especially touchy about job security. Although UBPW's international officials were in favor of the program concept, Dion felt that they weren't as concerned about the individual workers involved, and that it was his duty as their elected representative to protect their specific interests, especially job security.

Michaels, pressured by Peters, decided to pursue the employee involvement program without Dion's support. With the assistance of the IHR Committee, he held several informal meetings about the benefits of employee involvement, both with plant management and the rank and file. During the last of these meetings with the production employees, Dion stood at the back of the break-room, arms crossed, and listened patiently. At the end, when the discussion was opened to the floor, Dion spoke:

"Gene, I've got a mortgage, two cars, and my kid needs braces. How will your program help me if it's such a big success that I'm out of a job because of it?"

The meeting broke up with no further comments from the union members. When the contract expired, they voted unanimously to go out on strike. Negotiations with Dion were just reiterative of his comment the night of the meeting. After 30 days, however, he met informally with Michaels and expanded his argument.

"Gene, I've got—"

"I know, Landers, I know: mortgage, cars, and a kid with crooked teeth."

Dion slid his fingers over the pencil in his hand until they touched the table, flipped the pencil around, and slid his fingers down again. Michaels watched with irritation as Dion refused to speak.

"So what do you want me to do?" asked Michaels with exasperation.

Dion looked him straight in the eye and stopped toying with his pencil.

"Promise me that we all have a job."

EMPLOYEE INVOLVEMENT PROGRAM

While corporate refused an absolute no layoff clause, they agreed to the negotiation team's suggestion for a "Best Effort to Transfer" provision, which stated that Cynex would attempt to transfer any hourly displaced due to implementation of EIP recommendations. Furthermore, any unavoidably displaced workers were to be given 60 days advance notice. Local 819 agreed to EIP with the further provisions that the program would be strictly voluntary, and that the union contract was off limits. The workers returned on May 13th.

EIP came under the jurisdiction of corporate's Interactive Human Resource (IHR) program, active since the end of 1983. The IHR program established a three-tier organizational structure for EIP, similar to the one utilized at DataSync. The first tier was comprised of the plant steering committee. Michaels and Dion were appointed co-chairpersons of the steering committee, and they together selected and appointed five additional members: the general foreman, the production supervisor, the Local vice president, the Local secretary-treasurer, and a rotating member. The rotating member was elected by the union membership to serve on the steering committee for a two-month term. The only requirement was that a rotating member must have undergone EIP training prior to the election. The rotating membership allowed all six production departments (outside of New Products) to be represented on the steering committee in any given year. The steering committee was to meet weekly to discuss cross-departmental problems, provide technical resources to team leaders, and monitor the overall progress of EIP.

The steering committee members participated in the 40 hours of training provided by corporate for team members. This training involved learning problem-solving techniques, group dynamics, and presentation skills. Furthermore, they received an additional 20 hours of training in team building and problem resolution. The corporate human resource department also supplied Cynex with two program facilitators (both of whom underwent training with the steering committee members), with the understanding that any additional facilitators would be appointed from the Local union membership. These facilitators were charged with coordinating training of all team participants, to be conducted over a 10-week period during paid time. These facilitators also provided teams with technical advice and assisted teams in getting recommendations implemented. In the latter half of 1985, the steering committee appointed an additional facilitator from the union membership.

Following their training, the steering committee's first task was to solicit departmental participation in the EIP. The committee approached the Reman unit, which was responsible for the manufacture or remanufacture of replacement parts for Cynex's obsolete product lines. Their decision was based on the extreme cost-competitiveness within the replacement parts market, and the fact that this department had been the hardest hit by economic layoffs. They met with workers and supervisors from Reman during paid time to discuss the EIP and to solicit volunteers to undergo training. Twelve workers volunteered, all within labor grades of six or lower. The steering committee then established the Reman departmental committee.

Departmental committees formed the second tier of EIP, and were composed of the general foreman, department technical staff, an elected union official, and department team leaders. These committees, established as EIP expanded, were to meet weekly to develop plans for establishing and implementing employee involvement teams, monitor team activities, and coordinate various team activities across the department. The Reman departmental committee established the first two problem-solving teams.

Problem-solving teams comprised the third tier of the EIP. Six to eight hourly volunteer employees and their foreman or an elected team leader were to meet for about an hour each week to discuss ways to improve performance or the quality of worklife. By the end of the first year, nearly half of the 82 Reman hourly employees had completed training, and the steering committee established departmental committees for Mechanical Sub-Assembly and Floor Assembly.

Problem-solving teams were to focus on job-related problems and ways of improving company performance without violating contractual language. Permissible subjects included product quality, waste and scrappage, rework, health and safety, material and inventory costs, and improvements in facilities, tools, and equipment. One of the first suggestions to come out of team activities was that the restrooms be painted some color other than institutional green. Michaels became increasingly skeptical of EIP as similar suggestions followed over the first three or four months. Eventually, however, workers' suggestions for improved scheduling (traditionally supervisors' role), reducing waste, and materials handling began to have a measurable, favorable impact on the cost of production.

Recommendations costing less than $250 could be implemented with only supervisor approval. Recommendations costing between $250 and $2,500 were presented, with the assistance of facilitators, to the departmental committee. Approval was by consensus. Proposals approved, yet costing more than $2,500, were costed out by the departmental committee and submitted to the steering committee for final approval.

By 1987 there were 22 teams active within Reman, Mechanical Sub-Assembly, and Floor Assembly, and the steering committee was establishing departmental committees for Machine Shop Electrical Assembly and considering teams within the two maintenance units.

MAY 14, 1987

The Cynex team was now comprised of Michaels, Grant Young, director of labor relations at the facility, and Ward Ebers, Cynex's production manager. UBPW's team was comprised of Dion, Andy Clemons, vice president of Local 819, and Matt Ryan, head committeeman at the plant. These teams had come to consensus on most issues pertaining to the contract, including some reductions in job classifications (see Exhibits 6 and 7, pp. 76 and 77), yet the future of EIP was hanging in the balance. Michaels and Dion had met privately for dinner to discuss possible common interests in the remaining items under dispute.

"O.K.," Michaels opened, "why don't you tell me what you think we disagree on."

"We want EIP in New Products—"

"That's not an issue, Landers," Michaels interrupted, "Because we want it in New Products, too. But it's *not* going to work there unless we can ease up on the seniority provisions within the area. Those guys average two to three transfers a year, in and out of departments and areas, which keeps our employee relations staff up to their ears trying to rearrange everyone's schedule according to the contract, and then retraining everyone in their new job."

"Gene, how much blood do you expect out of this turnip? I'm not even sure the members will okay those reduced job classes. You just can't keep tearing into a contract like a bull in a china shop."

"But Landers, they're all over the plant. I'm not asking you to get rid of seniority, just, just—hell, just keeping them in their department would help."

"Well, I'd bet they'd stay put if they had a good reason," Dion replied.

"Ah, yes," Michaels sighed, "Your election platform."

"Now, Gene, that's not fair. Sure I've got my eye on the national elections, but profit sharing is fair for the workers. They've given Cynex a lot of their ideas and have nothing to show for it. Look at the wages for the next three years. If you won't give, why should we?"

"Landers, *that's* not fair. You know corporate is willing to consider gainsharing based on direct labor cost savings, but to demand profit sharing is to ask for a piece of the pie that you didn't help bake. Gainsharing wouldn't be such a bad idea if you'd let the best ideas from EIP get implemented."

"Once a bull, always a bull," Dion quipped.

"No, Landers," Michaels replied slowly, "In this day and age, that contract is NOT fine china; it's a death warrant—at least as far as keeping Cynex solvent so we all have jobs."

"Think so?"

"You bet I do."

"It's awful hard for my members to believe you when all you offer in return is the big guys' 'Best Effort'."

Michaels jaw clenched, "BET has worked very well within EIP. Nobody's been laid off because of program recommendations."

"How come 25 men who were working last year ain't working this year?"

"That had nothing to do with EIP; corporate cut distribution of the parts for TI77E."

"But we had EIP on the TI77E. Fat lot of good it did those 25 members."

"All of their big ideas conflicted with the contract. Layoffs or no layoffs, that contract is like a noose around EIP's neck. Besides, all workers have preferential hiring to other facilities."

"I always thought 'preference' meant something good," Dion stated dryly, "But here their choice is that they can uproot their families and move at least 500 miles away or play a 50–50 chance of ending up in a nonunion plant. And because management likes their plants nonunion, the members just become 'preferential' sitting ducks."

"Listen, we've got less than six hours to resolve this thing. Mull it over, and we'll have the negotiation teams meet again at 10:00 P.M. in my office, okay?"

Dion nodded, and stared silently at Michaels for a moment.

"Gene," he finally spoke, "You know I can't make the members accept what they don't want. You gotta do what you gotta do, but remember: I gotta do what I gotta do. Those are the rules of this game. If you start messing with the rules, you might as well rewrite the game."

Michaels reread the memo from Dave Peters, delivered by messenger that morning. He checked the time again: 10:10 P.M. They had a lot to discuss.

QUESTIONS

1. What does plant management want out of these negotiations? Corporate?
2. What are the interests of the union, and are they compatible with plant management interests? Corporate interests?
3. Given your answers to questions 1 and 2, what is your prognosis for the EI program?

EXHIBIT 1 Cynex Consolidated Income Account, 1984–1986 ($000 omitted)

	1986	1985	1984
Sales	150,289	154,284	141,136
Cost of sales	109,920	114,857	107,263
Selling expense	25,996	27,732	25,280
Operating income	14,373	11,695	8,593
Interest income	9,536	5,045	3,457
Total	23,909	16,740	12,050
Interest expense	2,135	2,990	1,778
Income taxes	10,016	6,325	4,725
Net income	**11,758**	**7,425**	**5,547**

EXHIBIT 2   Darbough-Jones 1986 Organizational Chart

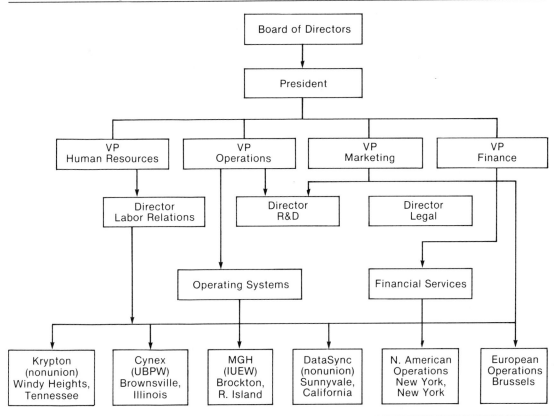

EXHIBIT 3 Cynex Organizational Chart

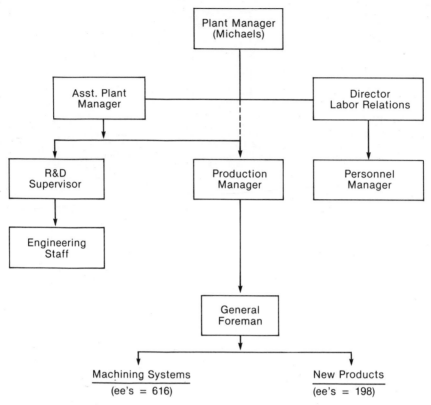

Machining Systems
(ee's = 616)

1. Mechanical Subassembly
2. Electrical Assembly
3. Machine Shop
4. Floor Assembly
5. Reman
6. Inspection

New Products
(ee's = 198)

7. Mech. Subassembly (NP)
8. Elec. Subassembly (NP)
9. Experimental
10. Expeditors
11. Inspection (NP)

(ee's = 46)

12. Maintenance-Electrical
13. Maintenance-Mechanical

EXHIBIT 4   Cynex Plant Job Classification

Classification	Labor Grade
Auto lathe (C)	9
Auto lathe (N/C)	10
Auto thread lathe	11
Auto weld-machine shop	9
Bench (C)	3
Blacksmith	11
Burning machine	8
Burning machine helper	4
Centering machine group	9
Centerless grinder (C)	5
Centerless grinder (N/C)	8
Clamp (MSA)	8
Clamp (NPA)	12,14
Clamp helper	7
Clean and paint	8
Controller parts assembly	11
Coordinate measuring machine	16
Cutter link set screw assembly (C)	3
Cylindrical grinder	10
Drill press (C)	6
Drill press (N/C)	11
Duplicator lathe	11
E. B. fusion weld (C)	6
Electrical inspector	17
Expeditor	10
Experimental mechanic	18
Final assembly	16
Final assembly and field inspector	17
Final mechanical inspector	17
Gear assembly	14
Gear hob and sprocket cutter	14
Horizontal boring machine (M)	15
Horizontal boring machine (N/C)	12
Horizontal boring machine (C)	8
Internal grinder	10
Janitor helper	1
Janitor	4
Jigmill (M)	14
Jigmill (N/C)	12
Jigmill (C)	7
Layout-machine shop	12
Machining center	14
Machine parts inspector	15
Machine wirer	16

EXHIBIT   4—*Continued*

Maintenance helper, electrical	10
Maintenance man, electrical	17
Maintenance helper, mechanical	9
Maintenance man, mechanical	15
Machine cell attendant (C)	7
Machine cell operator (C)	11
Milling machine (N/C)	10
Milling machine (C)	6
Molding press	6
NC machine tool repair	19
Numericenter	12
Panel assembly	13
Parts distribution	9
Parts transfer	6
Planer type mill	13
Power sweeper	2
Profiler	11
Radial drill press 3′ and 4′	10
Radial drill press 5′ and 6′	11
Semiauto drill machine (C)	7
Semiauto drill machine (N/C)	10
Robot welder attendant	13
Robot welder operator	14
Semiauto internal grinding machine (C)	5
Semiauto milling and drilling machine (C)	7
Semiauto pin drill (C)	5
Set up assembly	9
Set up assembly shuttle	11
Snag and grind	5
Speed drill press	5
Storekeeper (C)	10
Shop scheduling clerk (C)	12
Strippet and punch press	6
Sweeper	1
Surface grinder (M)	11
Surface grinder (N/C)	9
Surface grinder (C)	5
Tape horizontal drill	12
Template maker	10
Template storage	3
Tool crib attendant	9
Tool grinder attendant	15
Tool grinder	13
Tool maker	19
Tool room welder	17
Turning lathe	11

EXHIBIT　4—*Concluded*

Turret lathe and bar machine	12
Turret lathe (N/C)	12
Utilityman	2
Utilityman (C)	6
Utilityman (N/C)	3
Vertical band saw	6
Vertical shaper (C)	4
Vertical turret lathe (C)	10
Vertical turret lathe (N/C)	12
Warehouse person	11
Warehouse clean and paint	9
Wheelabrator and Olson furnace operator	6
Warehouse system operator	13

Note: MSA = Machining systems area
　　　NPA = New products area
　　　C　 = Computer controlled
　　　N/C = Numerically controlled
　　　M　 = Manually controlled

EXHIBIT 5　Union Wage Rates

Grade	Hourly Rate
1	$10.53
2	10.59
3	10.66
4	10.72
5	10.80
6	10.88
7	10.95
8	11.07
9	11.16
10	11.23
11	11.31
12	11.41
13	11.53
14	11.74
15	11.93
16	12.04
17	12.16
18	12.28
19	12.41
20	12.53

EXHIBIT 6 Tentative 1987 Key Contract Agreement (UBPW and Cynex)

Wages
- Lump sum payment of $1,000 first year; 2 percent second year; 2 percent third year.

Job Classifications
- Certain job classifications to be collapsed as indicated in Exhibit 7, representing 8 percent reduction in classifications.

Benefits
- Change to 80:20 copayment on health insurance; extend qualification period from one month to three months on long-term disability.
- Increase pension annuity from 1.5 percent to 1.6 percent of last five years average earnings (times years of service).

Holidays
- One additional personal holiday per year (total of two) in exchange for George Washington's birthday.

Transfer Rights
- Preferential hiring rights to other facilities for laid-off employees.

Advance Notice
- Thirty-day advance notice and consultation with union regarding technological changes to be introduced.

EXHIBIT 7   Tentative Revised Job Classification

Old Classification	Old Labor Grade	New Classification	New Labor Grade
Auto lathe (C)	9	Auto lathe (C/A)*	9
Auto lathe (N/C)	10		
Centerless grinder (C)	5	Centerless grinder (C/A)	6
Centerless grinder (N/C)	8		
Drill press (C)	6	Drill press (C/A)	8
Drill press (N/C)	11		
Horizontal boring machine (N/C)	12	Horizontal boring machine (C/A)	8
Horizontal boring machine (C)	8		
Jigmill (N/C)	12	Jigmill (C/A)	9
Jigmill (C)	7		
Milling machine (N/C)	10	Milling machine (C/A)	6
Milling machine (C)	6		
Surface grinder (N/C)	9	Surface grinder (C/A)	5
Surface grinder (C)	5		
Vertical turret lathe (C)	10	Vertical turret lathe (C/A)	11
Vertical turret lathe (N/C)	12		

*C/A = Computer assisted.

Appendix   Selected Contract Articles

Article 6
Seniority

A. Seniority Defined

Seniority is the credited service of the employee in the bargaining unit, beginning with the date on which the employee began to work, after last being hired, and subject to any adjustments under this Agreement. If two or more employees are hired on the same day, seniority shall be order of employee number, the lowest number being senior.

Employees shall not accumulate seniority rights until they have completed their probationary period; however, if an employee is continued in his employment after completing such probation period his seniority shall revert back to his starting date.

An employee shall cease to have seniority and his employment with the Company shall be considered terminated for all purposes when an employee:

    1. Voluntarily leaves the Company.

    2. Is discharged for just cause.

    3. Fails to report for work after having been jointly notified by the Union and the Company.

    4. Fails to return to work promptly following recovery from illness or injury.

B. Seniority Principle

The Company and the Union accept the principle of seniority and agree if qualifications and ability to perform the job are relatively the same between employees involved, the length of continuous service shall govern next on a facilitywide basis in cases of job openings (Article 11), transfers and promotions (Article 12), shift preferences (Article 16) and layoffs and recall (Article 19). The principle of seniority for vacation and overtime scheduling will apply only within individual departments.

Article 11
Job Openings: Postings

Whenever a vacancy occurs on a job with a classification in Labor Grade 2 or above, the Company will post such an opening on all bulletin boards, with a copy mailed to any employees on layoff and to a board member designated by the Union, indicating the job title, rate of pay, shift and qualifications required; provided, however, that no posting will be required when an employee is upgraded within his area of skill. Such notice shall remain on the bulletin boards for not less than three (3) working days before the job opening is filled, except that openings for the same kind of vacancies need not be posted within a thirty (30) day period after the closing time of the first posting. Any employee may be temporarily assigned to such opening during the time required to complete the above procedure. Any employee who wishes to transfer to a job opening posted on the bulletin board must fill out a Request for Transfer form at the Personnel Department on or before the closing date and hour specified on the posted notice or else the employee need not be considered for the opening. The closing date and hour will be a minimum of seventy-two (72) hours from the time the notice is posted.

Article 12
Transfers and Promotions

Employees may apply for a transfer to another position at any time prior to or during the time a job is posted by completing a Request for Transfer form, which shall remain in effect for six (6) months. Employees who file a request for transfer will be given consideration by the Company in compliance with the principles set forth in Article 6, Section B of this Agreement provided that an opening exists or a new job is created and such position involves a higher paying job or potentially higher paying job.

Article 16
Shift Preferences

The Company agrees to the principle that seniority should be given consideration when making shift assignments and the Company will assign employees on the basis of seniority to the shift of their preference when an opening occurs, provided such assignment does not interfere with production efficiency. The procedure within a department relating to shift changes within the department shall be posted in each department.

Article 19
Layoff and Recall

It is the intent of the Company to provide full and regular employment for its employees; however, if the Company determines a layoff is necessary the principle of seniority as defined in Article 6, Section B shall apply for purposes of layoff and recall. . . . Employees bumping less senior employees in the event of layoffs are entitled to the wage rate of their prior job classification for a period of six (6) months. Thereafter, employees will be paid according to the labor grade of the job classification he holds.

Louisiana-Pacific and the LPIW, Western Council

Louisiana-Pacific and 1,700 members of the Western Council of Lumber, Production, and Industrial Workers (LPIW) were enduring the sixth month of a bitter strike affecting 17 facilities in the Pacific Northwest. Strikers hurled stones; replacement workers assailed picketers. Gunshots and arson were reported. Once a company van rammed a group of strikers.

Negotiations between the company and the union had ceased, pending the Seattle NLRB Regional Office's decision regarding Louisiana-Pacific's alleged illegal activity during the strike. Specifically, the LPIW claimed that Louisiana-Pacific aided in the filing of decertification elections; unfairly circulated information directly to employees, circumventing union representation; and merely shadow-boxed throughout negotiations, offering counterproposals designed to frustrate, not progress, bargaining.

On December 29, 1983, the regional director denied the union's charges and refused to issue a complaint (see Exhibit 1, p. 89).

INDUSTRY BACKGROUND

The domestic forest products industry is dominated by three or four tiers of key players (see Exhibit 2, p. 90). At the first tier are the giants: Weyerhaeuser, Georgia-Pacific, Boise-Cascade, and Champion International. Broad-based companies, they own timberland, process lumber and pulp, and produce a variety of finished products. At the second

---

*This case was largely based upon information available through the National Labor Relations Board, Office of the General Counsel, per the Freedom of Information Act.

tier are such companies as Louisiana-Pacific, MacMillan Bloedel, and Potlatch, which offer narrower product lines and own only some of their timber requirements. At the third and fourth tiers are a variety of specialty producers, almost none of which own any timberland. Many of the second-, third-, and fourth-tier companies bid for cutting rights to government-owned land.

The industry historically shifts to wherever timber is plentiful. Starting in New England, the industry moved to the Great Lakes region in the late 1800s, then into the Pacific Northwest in the late 1920s. The Pacific Northwest timber region remained prosperous for over 50 years. Over time, however, the plentiful supply of trees diminished, forcing companies into more and more rugged terrain. Moreover, much of the land is now government-owned and subject to changing legislation affecting timberland use.

In 1982, transporting Northwest lumber products became more costly following passage of the Jones Act. Previously, bulk items such as timber were shipped from the West Coast to the East Coast via seaways on competing countries' vessels. The Jones Act, however, mandated that any product shipped between U.S. ports must be shipped on U.S.-made, -owned, and -operated vessels, at an appreciably higher cost. Using alternate rail transportation over the Rocky Mountains was equally expensive; it cost as much to transport a load of timber from Washington state to Arizona as to Osaka, Japan.

In contrast with the Northwest, the South boasted longer growing seasons, flat terrain, cheaper transportation costs, and worker wages about half the unionized rate in the Northwest. In the late 50s, timber was not even listed as a southern agricultural product; by 1980, six southern states listed timber as the number one agricultural product. In 1982, southern plywood production surpassed that of the Northwest.

Despite ongoing cost-reduction efforts, the 1982 recession financially devastated the domestic lumber industry. Housing starts plummeted as mortgage interest rates reached 18 percent, and companies within the $40 billion forest products industry reported operating losses for the first time since World War II. Moreover, the government-subsidized Canadian lumber companies had increased their U.S. market penetration to 30 percent.

In response to flat demand and Canadian competition, domestic companies reduced production capacity, permanently closing some of their least cost-efficient mills. Between 1980 and 1983, over 6,000 Northwest lumber workers were permanently laid off, driving the unemployment rate in some Northwest areas to 30 percent.

In the early 80s, one third of the 170,000 western lumber employees were union members, predominantly within the LPIW or International Woodworkers of America (IWA). As members of the Western Wood Products Association, the seven largest lumber companies (the first tier) bargained on a multiemployer basis, establishing the percentage-pattern for the industry. The second tier, although not active in bargaining, followed the pattern set by the Big Seven. The third tier, comprised of more than 50 small companies, bargained jointly through the Timber Operators Council, still under the shadow of the Big Seven pattern. In the words of LPIW's Executive Secretary James S. Bledsoe:

> Since 1958, and certainly since 1963, when we commenced our joint bargaining, we have had a position and a policy that the patterns, as they are created at the wealthiest tier, are passed down through the poorest. And, frankly, we've been very successful, if you ignore the fact that we have virtually struck 8,000 of our members out of work in order to create those patterns.
>
> I can show mill after mill, particularly in that fourth tier, where we have gone after the patterns have been set and said, "Here it is. Here's where you sign. No, we won't make any concessions. That's the pattern." They've signed. They've either gone out of business or they've taken the strike, and we've struck them out of business.[1]

LOUISIANA-PACIFIC BACKGROUND

In 1972, Georgia-Pacific formed and spun-off Louisiana-Pacific as part of an antitrust agreement with the Federal Trade Commission. Louisiana-Pacific, guided by former Georgia-Pacific manager Harry Merlo, head-quartered itself on one-and-a-half floors of a Portland, Oregon, office building. With the initial dowry of 20 percent of Georgia-Pacific's earning power and four executives, including the aggressive and resourceful Merlo, Louisiana-Pacific carved out a formidable niche in the lumber industry (see Exhibit 3, p. 90).

Many characterized Merlo as a lumber industry maverick. Moustached and often sporting a full-length fur coat, Merlo led Louisiana-Pacific against the industry grain. If the industry bought timberland, Merlo ordered timberland sold. When other lumber companies decided against plywood substitute production, Merlo committed to it. Obsessed with cost control, Merlo would cut a manager's salary by 20 percent if the manager's operation ran in the red.

Merlo would never admit defeat. In 1978 a Congressional vote expanded the Redwood National Park in northern California, forcing Louisiana-Pacific to sell over 25,000 acres of redwood timber in exchange for almost $225 million. Louisiana-Pacific contested the sale price, perpetuating the dispute through numerous court proceedings. Each annual report lists the disputed balance owing under "accounts receivable."

---

[1]James S. Bledsoe address to the 41st Annual Convention of the Western Council LPIW, Sacramento, California, March 14, 1983.

Merlo wanted Fibreboard Corporation's timber holdings and in 1978 purchased the company from Simkins Industry. Shortly after purchase, the Federal Trade Commission ordered the sale of one Fibreboard facility under antitrust allegations. While Louisiana-Pacific reduced total production output from the Fibreboard facilities, it failed to actually divest a plant. A federal judge, in turn, fined Louisiana-Pacific $4 million in December 1982 for failure to comply with the order. The company appealed the fine.

While battling the purchase aftermath, Louisiana-Pacific was brought up on fraud charges for how it arranged the purchase. Louisiana-Pacific allegedly issued false press releases stating that the sale fell through, depressing Fibreboard stock prices. Due to suspiciously erased tape recordings, missing documents, and conflicting company testimony, a jury found Louisiana-Pacific guilty of fraud in June 1982. The judge awarded Simkins Industries over $1 million, and another $4 million distributed among anyone owning or trading Fibreboard stock between January 25, and March 9, 1978.

A third litigious problem was inherited with the Fibreboard purchase. Fibreboard used asbestos in the production of certain insulation products until 1971. Louisiana-Pacific inherited the various class-action suits against such producers, which included Manville Corporation as the principal co-defendant. When Manville filed Chapter 11, it gained protection from pending lawsuits. As a result, remaining co-defendants, including Fibreboard, realized increased claims against them. In early 1983, a new class-action suit was filed against previous asbestos producers, seeking funded removal of asbestos from schools and other facilities. Totaled, Louisiana-Pacific acquired more than 40,000 pending lawsuits against Fibreboard.

Louisiana-Pacific's legal battles were not limited to the Fibreboard purchase. The company also waged an ongoing dispute with the Environmental Protection Agency regarding excessive waste-water discharges from its Samoa, California, pulp mill. The Justice Department filed the suit in 1978; Louisiana-Pacific requested a variance from the standard pollution limits. In November 1982, Louisiana-Pacific was found guilty of exceeding the limits and given 22 months to install waste-water treatment facilities at an estimated cost of $20 million. The company was also subject to civil penalties for the violation.

Louisiana-Pacific's colorful, litigious history, however, did not hurt company performance. Even during the 1982 recession when the company reported a net loss of $17 million, their balance sheet remained stable (see Exhibit 4, p. 91). And unlike other domestic competitors, only two facilities had been closed (see Exhibit 5, p. 92). That same year, Louisiana-Pacific also announced major capital investment activity, predominantly for production of waferwood, a reconstituted wood panel 30 percent cheaper to produce than plywood yet retailing just 15 percent below plywood prices.

1983 NEGOTIATIONS

While historically bargaining on a companywide basis, Louisiana-Pacific joined the Western Wood Products Association during 1980 contract negotiations. Wage and fringe benefits percentage increases were negotiated collectively for all locations, yet separate agreements were maintained at locations in Oregon, Washington, California, Idaho, and Montana. The contract called for increases of 9 percent, 8 percent, and 6.5 percent in each successive contract year. The agreements expired May 31, 1983, for all locations except Moyie Springs, Idaho (September 1, 1983), Trout Creek, Montana (October 1, 1983), and Truckee, California (November 30, 1983).

At the onset of 1983 negotiations, many workers were just returning to mills temporarily closed during 1982. Early in the talks, two companies withdrew from association bargaining, but indicated they would accept whatever agreement was reached. Merlo met with LPIW Executive Secretary Bledsoe in early 1983 to discuss gaining wage and fringe benefit parity with southern mills.[2] Merlo demanded wage rollbacks, which Bledsoe stated the union would not agree to. Merlo informed Bledsoe that he would achieve his demands with or without the union's acquiescence. On February 14, Louisiana-Pacific withdrew from the Western Wood Products Association.

In May, however, Merlo approached the association, urging that they support an 8–10 percent wage reduction for new hires and a reduction in the contract term. The association declined. One member executive noted, however, that while the association wouldn't support Merlo's demands, they would take full advantage of any gains he might single-handedly win.

As the 1983 LPIW-Association talks progressed, the union agreed to concessions given economic conditions. On June 6 the parties signed a new three-year contract which included a first-year wage freeze and subsequent-year wage increases of 4 percent and 4.5 percent. Although a concessionary contract, second-, third-, and fourth-tier companies resisted the pattern, with Louisiana-Pacific at the lead. The 1982 recession left many of these smaller companies vulnerable to flat demand, as well as outstanding government timber-cutting bid commitments made when demand was strong. Bledsoe acknowledged the difficulty of pattern bargaining for fourth-tier companies:

> I've got to tell you that in terms of our current situation, in terms of the current economy of the country, in terms of logic—[pattern bargaining] has not been a very smart policy. Now understand, so there's absolutely no doubt in your mind and no miscalculation, misjudgment about what I'm saying. I am talking

---

[2]At the time of the case, Louisiana-Pacific Pacific Northwest millworkers started at $9.90 an hour, earning up to $13.50 an hour; southern millworkers earned almost half that rate.

about the fourth tier. I'm not talking about the second and third. The first one will take care of itself, because that's the pattern-setter.

Some accommodations may have to be made for the fourth tier. Some accommodation was made, as a matter of fact, in 1980 for some of them. Some of them, in spite of the accommodation, went under.[3]

Louisiana-Pacific demanded unit-by-unit bargaining, which prompted the LPIW to file unfair labor practice charges against Louisiana-Pacific. The company argued that 18 separate facilities were contained within four operating divisions; only the Coastal Division's five facilities had a multiplant agreement. The other facilities' contracts varied greatly in terms of wages, hours, working conditions, and pension and medical benefits. The union countered that only percentage increases were applied across facilities, with the many individual unit wage rates normally varying, and that the small LPIW negotiation team (two persons) found unit-by-unit bargaining draining upon union resources. Pending a decision on the filed charge, however, LPIW began meeting with Louisiana-Pacific representatives at their various facilities.[4]

The first such meeting was held May 17, 1983, in Ketchikan, Alaska.[5] The union's opening proposal was identical to its proposal to the association. Louisiana-Pacific countered with wage cuts of over 10 percent for all employees currently on the payroll, a 20 percent reduction in wages for any new employees (i.e., a two-tier system), and significant rollbacks in fringe benefits, including holidays, vacations, and health care. The company also demanded the elimination of the cook house, which would have resulted in workers having no place to eat. Moreover, Louisiana-Pacific began requesting varying contract expiration dates (one year, 18 months, two years or three years), ultimately staggering the dates for future plant-by-plant bargaining.

Subsequent meetings were held in Sacramento, California (May 23); Eureka, California (May 24 and June 14); Klamath Falls, Oregon (June 15); Oroville, California (June 16); Standard, California (June 20); and Tacoma, Washington (June 21). At each meeting, the company negotiated the same rollbacks sought in Alaska, in addition to varying local changes. During Tacoma, Washington meetings, the company also expressed interest in reducing several semiskilled and skilled jobs. In the course of these unit negotiations, Louisiana-Pacific claimed it amended its existing employee wage concession to 7.5 percent, still within a two-tier system, for six facilities. This amendment, however, was not documented.

On June 24, 1983, in Sacramento, California, the company offered to freeze wages for current employees, but reduce new-hire wages and

---

[3]Bledsoe, March 14, 1983.

[4]Ultimately the regional office of the NLRB remanded the issue back to the parties, claiming that definition of the bargaining unit was a matter for negotiation.

[5]Ketchikan is represented by the IWA, but IWA and LPIW historically bargain jointly.

benefits (primarily medical insurance and holidays). The union and Louisiana-Pacific reached impasse, and over 1,500 LPIW and IWA lumberworkers walked out of those plants where contracts had expired. The union also organized "stranger" picket lines at Trout Creek, Montana and Truckee, California facilities, where contracts had not yet expired.

On July 18, the company made a new offer, viewed as significantly worse by the union. The new-hire wage reduction was increased from the previous 20 percent to 25 percent. New hires also would forego health and welfare payments, holiday pay, and vacations. Moreover, when new employees advanced to higher classifications, they would continue receiving entry-level wages, instead of moving to higher pay rates as originally proposed. Another new requirement was a 1,200-hour eligibility for vacation pay. The company argued that this proposal was not regressive but obviously and dramatically eliminated "all negative features affecting the striking employees."[6]

In July, Louisiana-Pacific announced they would lease and operate a sawmill in order to blunt the effects of the strike; seven of the struck facilities were operating with salaried and newly hired employees. Incidents of violence increased. One new hire smashed the strikers' tables and chairs with a baseball bat. Rock-throwing strikers in California were rammed by a company van.

The parties met on August 4 in Moyie Springs, Idaho, where the contract expired September 1. At the onset of negotiations, a Louisiana-Pacific representative handed the union a letter stating that it was closing down portions of the Moyie Springs operations. Then the company proposed an agreement significantly altering local working conditions, a proposal the union deemed, "the worst in any location to date, virtually emasculating the total working agreement. . . . making this a total management-oriented operation."[7]

The September 8 meeting regarding the Trout Creek, Montana facility made no negotiation headway. The union declared an impasse, and the workers went out on strike.

On September 16 in Pilot Rock, Oregon, the union modified its proposal, including (1) extension of the current contract for one year without any increase in wages; (2) agreement to the company-sponsored health and welfare program, so long as it remained jointly administered; and (3) that all strikers return to their previous positions without loss of seniority. Following the union's offer, Louisiana-Pacific negotiators requested an adjournment, with negotiations to reconvene at 7:30 that

---

[6]Company letter dated March 26, 1984, to the NLRB General Counsel (NLRB file #2.A), p. 8.

[7]Brief to the General Counsel in re: NLRB Case Nos. 19-CA-16243, 20-CA-18452, and 32-CA-5996; January 10, 1984, p. 9.

evening in Portland, Oregon. Several hours later, the company canceled the meeting, indicating they would reply to the offer the following Monday or Tuesday.

On September 22, the parties met in Klamath Falls, Oregon, and Louisiana-Pacific responded with a counterproposal that altered three provisions of its earlier proposal: two additional holidays for new hires; that the union relinquish its right to honor stranger picket lines; and elimination of a dues checkoff system.

The company rationale for rejecting the union's newest counteroffer was based on the following:

1. That the wage freeze for current employees under a current contract extension would not reduce new-hire wages, and thus not allow Louisiana-Pacific to reduce labor cost in an effort to establish parity with their southern facilities.

2. That a jointly administered health and welfare program, even though presumably company-sponsored, did not allow management freedom on such issues as choice of the insurance carrier.

3. That returning all strikers to their prestrike positions would force termination of the strike replacements, resulting in Louisiana-Pacific's "loss of credibility in the communities where strike replacements had undergone threats, hostility, and physical abuse in order to allow L-P to continue its operations."[8]

By October, Louisiana-Pacific was operating at 85 percent capacity in 15 of the 17 struck facilities, using both new hires and workers that crossed the picket lines. The company estimated that the strike had cost them $18 million in the third quarter, including $5 million for increased security.

On October 10, during a meeting in Eureka, California, Louisiana-Pacific requested the rewriting of a contract clause that penalized seniority rights of workers who had resigned their union membership in order to cross the picket line without fines. The company admitted that the latest offers "did contain some features which were less desirable from the union's standpoint, but they also contained additional features which were more desirable."[9] The union construed the two additional new-hire holidays as mere tokens, with the offer's union security eliminations highlighting the company's true union-busting purpose.

On October 21, a company spokesperson stated during a news interview for a local Portland television station:

"Our view is that if we could have the perfect world, we would go back to the work ethics of the 20s and 30s when that European full day's

---

[8]Company letter dated March 26, 1984, to the NLRB General Counsel (NLRB file #2.A), p. 10.
[9]Ibid. p. 8.

work for a full day's pay was not only the right but the privilege of individuals and get everybody thinking about individual performance again, rather than this mass collective protectionism."

On October 25, 1983, the union filed a complaint with the NLRB Seattle Regional Office, claiming that Louisiana-Pacific failed to bargain in good faith. In early December, counsel for the union met with Region 19 to highlight their allegations. Counsel stated that the September 16 and 22 meetings were the strongest indicia of bad faith, wherein Louisiana-Pacific placed new, yet significant, noneconomic issues upon the table in a preconceived effort to frustrate bargaining. Union counsel asserted that the law requires something more than a willingness to physically attend meetings. Quoting an earlier National Labor Relations Board decision:

> Viewed against this background of employer intent to frustrate bargaining, Respondent's conduct in negotiations takes on transparent meaning. Respondent made no concessions of any significance, and its bargaining posture remained fixed in all substantial particulars. The mere fact that Respondent met and talked with the Union is of no consequence in the circumstances. "[T]o sit at a bargaining table, or to sit almost forever, or to make concessions here and there, could be the very means by which to conceal a purposeful strategy to make bargaining futile or fail.[10]

The Seattle regional director dismissed the charges against Louisiana-Pacific, however, stating that:

"The investigation revealed that based upon the [Union's] evidence, the Charge does not support a prima facie violation of the Act. More specifically, our investigation disclosed that the Employer had modified its contract proposals regarding the various plants involved throughout the course of bargaining . . ."

QUESTIONS

1. What favored management during negotiations and the subsequent strike? What favored the union?
2. As a union leader, what would your strategy be now?

---

[10]*NLRB* v. *Herman Sausage Company, Inc.*, 275 F.2d 229, 232 (5th Cir. 1960). (244 NLRB at 273).

EXHIBIT 1

United States Government

NATIONAL LABOR RELATIONS BOARD

Region 19

29th Floor, Federal Building, 915 Second Avenue

Seattle, WA 98174

December 29, 1983

Mr. Bernard Jolles, Attorney
JOLLES, SOKOL & BERNSTEIN
721 SW Oak Street
Portland, Oregon 97205

Re: Louisiana Pacific Corporation
   Case Nos. 19-CA-16243
       20-CA-18452
       32-CA-5996

Dear Mr. Jolles:

The above-captioned case(s), charging violations under Section 8 of the National Labor Relations Act, as amended, (have) been carefully investigated and considered.

As a result of the investigation, it appears that further proceedings are not warranted at this time. I am, therefore, refusing to issue Complaint in this matter. A written summary report of the basis for my conclusions is attached.

Pursuant to the National Labor Relations Board Rules and Regulations, Series 8, as amended, you may obtain a review of this action by filing an appeal with the General Counsel addressed to the Office of Appeals, National Labor Relations Board, Washington, D.C. 20570, and a copy with me. This appeal must contain a complete statement setting forth the facts and reasons upon which it is based. The appeal must be received by the General Counsel in Washington, D.C. by the close of business on January 11, 1984.
Upon good cause shown, however, the General Counsel may grant special permission for a longer period within which to file. Any request for extension of time must be submitted to the Office of Appeals in Washington, and a copy of any such request should be submitted to me.

If you file an appeal, please complete the Form NLRB-4767, Notice of Appeal, I have enclosed with this letter and send one copy of the form to each of the other parties whose names and addresses are listed below. The notice forms should be mailed at the same time you file the appeal, but mailing the notice forms does not relieve you of the necessity for filing the appeal itself with the General Counsel and a copy of the appeal with the Regional Director within the time stated above.

      Very truly yours,

      John D. Nelson
      Regional Director

EXHIBIT 2   Domestic Forest Product Companies

Company	Operating Revenues (billions of dollars)			
	1980	1981	1982	1983
Georgia-Pacific	5.0	5.4	5.4	6.5
Weyerhaeuser	4.5	4.5	4.2	4.9
Champion International	3.8	4.1	3.7	4.2
Boise-Cascade	3.1	3.1	2.9	3.5
Louisiana-Pacific	1.2	1.0	0.9	1.1
MacMillan Bloedel	2.0	1.9	1.5	1.6
Potlatch Corporation	0.8	0.9	0.8	0.9
Triangle Pacific	0.2	0.2	0.2	0.2
Pope & Talbot	0.2	0.2	0.3	0.3

Company	Net Income (millions of dollars)			
	1980	1981	1982	1983
Georgia-Pacific	244	160	52	105
Weyerhaeuser	321	234	140	205
Champion International	182	120	40	82
Boise-Cascade	136	120	7	60
Louisiana-Pacific	60	26	−17	28
MacMillan Bloedel	95	−23	−76	2
Potlatch Corporation	49	58	23	41
Triangle Pacific	3	5	5	11
Pope & Talbot	11	3	4	11

EXHIBIT 3   Louisiana-Pacific Product Mix (as percent of sales)

Product	1977	1978	1979	1980	1981	1982	1983
Redwood lumber	13%	9%	6%	5%	5%	4%	5%
Other lumber	42	46	47	38	35	32	38
Panel products	20	22	17	18	20	21	24
Logs, chips, misc.	12	11	13	18	19	22	18
Building total	87	88	83	79	79	79	85
Pulp	13	8	10	14	13	12	8
Paperboard/ containers	–	4	7	7	8	9	7
Paper total	13	12	17	21	21	21	15
Total	100%	100%	100%	100%	100%	100%	100%

Source: 1983 Annual report.

EXHIBIT 4 Louisiana-Pacific Balance Sheet December 31, 1982 (thousands omitted)

Assets

Current assets:

Cash and cash equivalents	$ 13,550	
Accounts receivable, less reserves	63,200	
Income taxes receivable	17,760	
Inventory	108,000	
Prepaid expenses	3,490	
Total current assets		$ 206,000
Timber and timberlands	177,680	
Receivable from U.S. government	214,900	
Property, plant, and equipment	584,010	
Investments and other assets	59,200	
Total assets		$1,241,790

Liabilities

Current liabilities:

Current portion of long-term debt	16,820	
Accounts payable	79,480	
Short-term notes payable	13,540	
Income taxes payable	–	
Total current liabilities		$ 109,840
Long-term debt	193,300	
Pension obligations/acquisitions	4,170	
Deferred income taxes	215,330	
Employee stock ownership plans	3,640	
Total liabilities		$ 518,470

Shareholders equity

Common stock at par value	32,020	
Additional paid-in capital	230,810	
Retained earnings	461,860	
Less treasury stock at cost	(1,370)	
Total shareholders equity		723,320
Total liabilities and shareholders equity		$1,241,790

Source: 1982 Annual report.

EXHIBIT 5   Louisiana-Pacific Manufacturing Facilities, 1982

Product	State	Number of plants	Normal Capacity (in board feet)
Sawmills	Alaska	2	130,000,000
	California	18	890,000,000
	Florida	3	135,000,000
	Idaho	6	215,000,000
	Louisiana	3	75,000,000
	Michigan	2	10,000,000
	Montana	3	105,000,000
	North Carolina	5	95,000,000
	Oregon	5	160,000,000
	Texas	7	180,000,000
	Washington	3	110,000,000
	Wyoming	2	30,000,000
	British Columbia	1	(closed)
Plywood	California	2	135,000,000
	Louisiana	1	175,000,000
	Oregon	1	(closed)
	Texas	2	285,000,000
Waferwood	Maine	1	130,000,000
	Texas	1	120,000,000
	Wisconsin	1	250,000,000
Other wood	Alabama	1	60,000,000
	California	4	390,000,000
	Louisiana	1	80,000,000
	Montana	1	100,000,000
	Wisconsin	2	190,000,000
Total lumber capacity		79	4,095,000,000
Paper and other products		21	

Source: 1982 Annual Report.

Contract Administration

Hartford Police Union

Under the Municipal Employees Relations Act, grooming standards are a mandatory subject of bargaining for municipal employees throughout Connecticut. In accordance with this act, Article VI, Section 6.11 of the bargaining agreement between the City of Hartford and the Hartford Police Union effective October 24, 1984, through October 23, 1987, empowered the chief of police to determine reasonable appearance standards applicable and binding on bargaining unit members effective July 1, 1985.

The three-year incumbant chief of police issued Order Number 6–15 establishing grooming policy and procedure. Included in the order was Procedure 3 stating that facial hair "other than mustaches, shall be prohibited." The chief claimed beards to be unprofessional for a paramilitary organization, undermining both esprit de corps and the neutral image necessary for public servants. Further, the chief contended that beards posed a potential safety hazard in the line of duty. The union grieved that Procedure 3 was an unreasonable grooming standard given that more than 20 officers had been wearing beards for several years, with no evidence that the chief's contentions were valid.

GROOMING STANDARDS FOR PUBLIC SERVANTS

In 1971, Hartford's department of personnel addressed the reasonableness of grooming standards following a patrolman's discharge for failure to comply with an order to cut his hair. While the in-force 1969 standards clearly limited hair growth and also forbade beards, the department reasoned that:

---

*This case was based in part on a 1986 Connecticut State Board of Mediation and Arbitration decision.

"The current regulations, when established in 1969, were reasonable and proper for the conditions applying at that time. Due to changing social standards during the interim, it does not appear that present regulations are enforceable at this time in their present form and will not support a dismissal for just cause. . . ."

However, while acknowledging that current social standards affect portions of the grooming standard, the department of personnel also indicated there remained "a proper and legitimate need for reasonable regulations appropriately related to the safety, internal discipline, and genuine public image of the police department."[1]

In 1973, a circuit court remanded a case back to the district court for summarily dismissing a patrolman's civil rights action seeking to invalidate hair grooming regulations of a country police department (*Dwen* v. *Barry*, 483 F.2d 1126). The circuit court noted that while numerous courts had upheld such regulations on the grounds that police organizations were paramilitary groups requiring strict discipline and uniformity in appearance, that such

> characterization is hardly justified either historically or functionally. . . . [A]ny "paramilitarism" of the force stems not from its origin nor from the nature of its duty but from the adoption of an organization with a centralized administration. . . . The use of such organization evolved as a practical administrative solution and not out of any desire to create a military force. . . . It is still locally controlled and organized, and subject to more direct control of the electorate. . . . [I]t has been suggested that the military model of organization and discipline must not be followed too closely as a policeman unlike a soldier frequently acts individually on his own initiative and not subject to the immediate supervision of his superiors.

Regarding personal infringement, the court continued:

> This is not to say, however, that the special nature of the police officer's duties and the recognized need to maintain a singular degree of discipline are immaterial. . . . A policeman does not, however, waive his right to be free from arbitrary and unjustifiable infringement of his personal liberty when he elects to join the force. . . . The question is whether the government may interfere with the physical integrity of the individual and require compliance with its standard or personal appearance without demonstrating some legitimate state interest reasonably requiring such restriction on the individual. The first, third, fourth, seventh, and eighth circuits have held that the Constitution limits the state's right to regulate the personal appearance of its citizens. We [the second circuit] agree.

In 1976, the Supreme Court in *Kelley* v. *Johnson* grappled with whether grooming standards regarding hair length imposed upon a public ser-

---

[1]It was shortly after the disposition of this grievance that several police officers began to grow beards.

vant's rights guaranteed under the Fourteenth Amendment. As did Hartford's department of personnel and the numerous circuit courts, the Supreme Court heavily weighed the reasons for such grooming standards, claiming that the key question was "whether respondent (police officer) can demonstrate that there is no rational connection between the regulation, based as it is on the county's method of organizing its police force, and the promotion of safety of persons and property."

The Court went on to state:

> Neither this Court, the Court of Appeals, nor the District Court is in a position to weigh the policy arguments in favor of and against a rule regulating hairstyles as a part of regulations governing a uniformed civilian service. The constitutional issue to be decided by these courts is whether petitioner's determination that such regulations should be enacted is so irrational that it may be branded "arbitrary," and therefore a deprivation of respondent's "liberty" interest in freedom to choose his own hairstyle. . . . [However], The overwhelming majority of state and local police in the present day are uniformed. This fact itself testifies . . . that similarity in appearance of police officers is desirable. This choice may be based on a desire to make police officers readily recognizable to the members of the public, or a desire for the esprit de corps which such similarity is felt to inculcate within the police force itself. Either one is a sufficiently rational justification for regulations. . . .

The *Kelley* decision prevailed in *Nalley* v. *Douglas County*, 498 F.Supp 1228 (1980), when a county road worker was dismissed for refusing to shave off his winter beard following implementation of a new grooming code. The county argued that the regulation fostered a uniform, desirable appearance to the public, and limited safety hazards, arguments supported by the *Kelley* decision. However, the court reasoned:

> As the instant regulation would be constitutional if applied to policemen and other public servants whose roles are subsumed by the *Kelley* decision the court will not strike it down for facial overbreadth. Rather, it merely holds that as applied to plaintiff Nalley, the regulation impermissibly restricted his protected rights to expression and personal liberty. When his interest is weighed against the county's wish to have its road maintenance crews present a uniformly clean-shaven appearance to taxpayers the constitutional safeguards prevail. It was evident from the transcript of the review hearing that uniforms for road workers are subsidized by the county but not required, indicating that the asserted goals of uniformity are not highly prized even by the enacters of the regulation. . . . The question of employee safety presents a more difficult question as the goal of preventing injury is less illusory. . . . In light of the type of work involved and the fact that the weight of proof favors [Nalley], the court determines that the slight degree, if any, to which the rule may further safety of road workers is outweighed by the infringement of Nalley's rights.

In a 1984 arbitration decision, also citing *Kelley* as controlling, an arbitrator found that a jail commissary storekeeper was properly ordered to shave his beard in an effort to foster a neutral image and sense of equality between inmates and jail personnel.

THE CITY'S POSITION

The city maintained that Order Number 6–15 was a reasonable appearance standard for reasons of neatness, image, uniformity, esprit de corps, and safety. The chief of police equated the police department with a paramilitary organization. Thus, it was critical that its members be readily identifiable and present a professional as well as neutral image to the public. Moreover, the chief contended that certain standards foster esprit de corps both within the organization and within the community. Finally, beards represented an additional appendage by which an officer could be grabbed, and thus represented a personal safety hazard for officers sporting them.

Citing *Kelley,* the city claimed that Order Number 6–15 was justified given the desirability of a uniform appearance among police officers, and therefore did not violate any officers' liberty rights under the Fourteenth Amendment. Because of the special nature of police organizations, acceptable social appearance standards for civilian professionals such as doctors, lawyers, educators, and politicians did not apply. The city further contended that it was extremely doubtful or even desirable for such individuals to strive for an esprit de corps that is central to a police force. Moreover, such civilians have no need to be concerned with the safety hazard beards may pose. The city acknowledged, however, that certain individuals have a medical reason for growing a beard; in such cases, a medical waiver could be secured, but such exceptions need not undermine the goal of the proposed regulation.

The city did not feel that blanket application of the 1971 Hartford Department of Personnel ruling was warranted for several reasons. First, the 1971 ruling dealt specifically with 1969 grooming standards. No grooming standards were in force until the last contract negotiations, which resulted in Article VI. During negotiations on Article VI, neither side raised or discussed the department of personnel's ruling as pertinent to or controlling the definition of "reasonable." Had this been the controlling standard, it should have been explicitly referenced in the contract. Also, since the time of that decision, numerous other grooming standards cases had been decided by higher authority, most notably the *Kelley* Supreme Court decision, giving weight to the chief of police's aims in promulgating the new grooming code prohibiting beards.

In summary, the city stated:

The parties empowered the chief of police to adopt effective July 1, 1985, *reasonable appearance standards,* which shall be applicable and binding on bargaining unit members. That certainly constitutes an agreed delegation of reasonable discretion to the Chief. In reviewing the exercise of such bargained for and delegated authority; a finding of abuse must be based on a conclusion that the adopted standard is so unusual as to be incapable of following within the broad parameters of the rule of reason. The Union, having agreed to grant the Chief such authority may not now attempt to substitute its judgment as to style or taste. In conclusion, the City respectfully urges the Panel to find that the order prohibiting beards is a reasonable grooming standard.

THE UNION'S POSITION

The Union did not dispute the chief of police's obligation to set forth grooming standards per the collective bargaining agreement. The union did, however, contend that Order Number 6–15 was not "reasonable" per the wording of Section 6.11 of the agreement, and arbitrary in light of the Hartford Department of Personnel's 1971 ruling. As such, per the *Kelley* decision, the rule was therefore a deprivation of officers' liberty interests. The burden to prove otherwise and substantiate reasons for the order rested solely on the city.

In contradicting the presumed necessity for such an order, the union argued that the police force was not a paramilitary organization demanding similarity in appearance among its members, per *Dwen* v. *Barry*. Further, unlike *Dwen*, the Hartford Department of Personnel had already mandated the terms under which any contractual grooming standard should be enacted per its 1971 arbitration decision; to wit, according to prevailing social acceptance. Numerous doctors, lawyers, executives, politicians, educators, and other professionals commonly grow beards, indicating the widespread social and professional acceptance of beards.

Given the widespread acceptance of beards, the union questioned the chief's claims of decreased esprit de corps. Moreover, the union, not the chief of police, was the representative of the majority of the police force, and the union was objecting to the provision. Thus, enactment of the provision might actually serve to decrease, not increase, esprit de corps.

The union also dismissed the potential safety hazard of a groomed beard based upon the 14-year presence of beards on the force with no such reports. In addition, the chief of police's order allowed hair for both men and women to extend to the top of the shoulder. Shoulder-length hair was a significantly longer "appendage" to be grabbed than a one-inch beard.

In summary, the union asserted:

Three Chiefs of Police before the present Chief of Police were not concerned about beards. What distinguishes this case from the vast majority of other grooming and, specifically, beard cases, is that the panel has the benefit of 14 years of experience with beards in the Hartford Police Department. There is absolutely nothing in the record with the exception of some unidentified, undated and undocumented complaints alluded to by the Chief of Police which suggests that the presence of beards on Hartford Police Officers has had any adverse impact on the department or its members. The inescapable conclusion here is that the Chief of Police simply does not like the appearance of beards himself. The Union has proposed to the Chief of Police that he promulgate a regulation which, while it would permit beards, would limit them in terms of length, cleanliness, etc. The Union submits that the City has not demonstrated the reasonableness of the proposed prohibition on beards and, accordingly, the regulation should be withdrawn.

QUESTION

Is the regulation reasonable? Why or why not?

Oil, Chemical & Atomic Workers and Day & Zimmerman

The Kansas Division of Day & Zimmerman, Inc. in Parsons, Kansas, manufactures ammunition and highly sensitive explosives for the United States Army. The Oil, Chemical & Atomic Workers International Union Local 5–508 represents approximately 800 production and maintenance workers at the Parsons facility. Six other bargaining units represent the remaining 500 workers.

In July 1985, an army major general contacted the Day & Zimmerman corporate offices, requesting that the company develop a chemical screening of all employees involved in sensitive areas, with mandatory counseling referral for discovered abusers. In turn, the director of industrial relations at the Parsons plant was charged with developing such a program.

On August 27, Local 5–508 formally objected to the unilateral implementation of any drug and alcohol abuse program without proper negotiations and agreement from the union. Over the next several months, the company developed its drug screening program after much consultation with employees, union representatives, and substance abuse counseling experts. On December 18, 1985, mandatory drug screening began for all employees, although no such screening program was developed for alcohol abuse. On March 28, 1986, a provision for the program was included in the prime contract between the Army and the plant.

---

*This case was based upon a 1987 Federal Mediation and Conciliation Service case.

DRUG ABUSE SCREENING AND TESTING PROGRAM

Prior to implementing the mandatory drug testing procedure, Day & Zimmerman already addressed employee use of narcotics under contractual "Rules of Conduct for Employees." According to Group I, Section 1.9 of these rules, discharge was the standard penalty for any employee entering or being on the plant site under the influence of marijuana or narcotics, or having any such substances in their possession.

The new program became Group VI of "Rules of Conduct for Employees." Pertinent sections of Group VI follow.

Group VI
Drug Abuse Screening and Testing Program

6.1(a) The Company has, pursuant to the directions of the U.S. Army, established a drug abuse screening and testing program for all employees. Under this program the Company's trained hospital staff will, during each workday, test a number of employees selected by badge number by a computerized random selection process.

(b) It is planned that all employees will be tested at least once in each six (6) month period.

(c) All new hires or employees recalled from layoff or returning from lengthy leaves of absence will be tested prior to being allowed to go to work.

6.2(b) The purpose of such immediate drug abuse testing of any such employee is to establish a baseline for future drug abuse testing and evaluation of the progress of such employee in dealing with such drug abuse problem.

(c) Such an employee may be required to undergo a drug abuse counseling program which has been approved by the Company's Medical Director or the Company's drug/alcohol abuse counselor, and the failure of an employee to comply with such counseling program will be just cause for disciplinary action up to and including discharge.

(d) Should future drug abuse testing of any such employee properly confirmed by an independent laboratory selected by the Company, reveal an increase in the level of the presence of a prohibited or an illegal drug in the body of such employee, this increase will be just cause for disciplinary action up to and including discharge.

6.3 Any employee . . . who is shown by the random drug abuse testing by the Company's hospital staff to have the presence of a prohibited or an illegal drug in his or her body will have such test reviewed and either confirmed or nullified by an independent laboratory selected by the Company.

6.4 Should the independent laboratory selected by the Company confirm the presence of a prohibited or an illegal drug in the body of an employee, other than an employee who has successfully undergone treatment for drug abuse or who is in the process of a successful drug abuse treatment and counseling program, such employee will be subject to the following actions by the Company:

(a) Such employee will receive a five (5) day disciplinary suspension and will be required to undergo a drug abuse counseling program which has been approved by the Company's Medical Director or by the Company's drug/alcohol abuse counselor.

(b) Any such employee who fails to comply with such mandatory drug abuse counseling program will be subject to further disciplinary action up to and including discharge.

(c) Any such employee will be tested on a regular basis to insure that the drug level present in his or her body continues to diminish. Should the drug level present in the body of such employee fail to diminish, the employee will be subject to further disciplinary action up to and including discharge.

In September of 1985, the army complained that the plant had no full-time drug and alcohol counselor, something they considered an integral part of the drug screening program. Day & Zimmerman indicated that they would contract with Labette Center for Mental Health to engage such a counselor for two to four hours per day. As of mid-1987, no such arrangement had been made.

DRUG TESTING PROCEDURE

The testing procedure involved analysis of employees' urine. First, any employee as defined within the Group VI requirements undergoing testing reports to the plant medical department. There the employee signs a form stating that he or she will not attempt to adulterate the urine sample. The employee then selects a specimen container and voids in the restroom with no other personnel present. Afterwards, the employee hands the container to the medical department technician, and the test is run in the employee's presence. Exhibit 1 (see p. 108) outlines procedural protocol following results of the first test.

URINALYSIS

There are two basic ways to test for the presence of drug metabolites in the urine: by analyzing chemical reactions of metabolites to enzymes (the immunoassay method), or by analyzing molecular configurations of metabolites (thin layer chromatography or GC/Mass Spectrometry). Enzyme immunoassays measure the amount of light given off in chemical reactions between an enzyme, an antibody, and the drug being tested for. Day & Zimmerman's medical department used the popular Syva Emit® system. Syva offers kits selling in the range of $6 to $11 to test for 11 different drugs. The technique is popular in private industry because it can be conducted by any trained personnel, thus eliminating the need for licensed laboratory technicians.

The Syva Emit® assay kit for detecting marijuana is a two-step microanalysis, detecting the presence of 11-nor-$\triangle^9$-THC-9-carboxylic acid, the major urinary metabolite of marijuana's psychoactive ingredient, $\triangle^9$-THC. Within the first 72 hours after drug ingestion, only 50 percent of the drug metabolites are excreted; the remaining are very slowly excreted over time. Because of this excretion pattern, company literature on the test states the following:

> Because psychoactive effects do not correlate with urinary metabolite levels and because of variations in absorption, distribution, method of ingestion, and urinary volume, a positive result from the assay of urinary $\triangle^9$-THC metabolites indicates only the presence of cannabinoids and does not indicate or measure intoxication.[1]

Regarding the accuracy of the technique, Syva reports that when the reagents (combining chemicals) and samples are stored between two degrees and eight degrees centigrade, identification is 99 percent accurate. However, this accuracy rate is contingent upon ideal laboratory conditions. Human error, equipment malfunction, and improper specimen handling can increase the likelihood of inaccuracy. Several independent studies retesting privately conducted tests gave false positive error rates of anywhere from 25 to 60 percent.[2]

Beyond these administering difficulties, the test methodology has been criticized as claiming positive results due to ingestion of other noncontrolled substances. In February 1986, Syva notified customers that three nonsteroidal anti-inflammatory drugs (ibuprofen, fenoprofen, and naproxen) produce positive Emit® marijuana results. Two popular over-the-counter aspirin substitutes contain ibuprofen. Moreover, ingestion of over-the-counter cold remedies has resulted in a test positive for amphetamines; Thorazine tests positive as heroin; and certain antibiotics test positive as cocaine.[3]

As a result of these testing anomolies, Syva and other immunoassay technique manufacturers strongly urge that any positive test via immunoassay be confirmed by alternate scientific methods, including gas chromatography/mass spectometry, considered the most sensitive and specific method. In GC/Mass Spectometry, the urine sample is broken down into individual ions so that the drug's molecular configuration can be analyzed. As molecular configurations are unique, this method is virtually 100 percent accurate. It is also extremely expensive, ranging from $60 to $100 per sample.

Another dilemma in conducting immunoassay and confirming GC/Mass Spectometry is that a single lab seldom performs both types of tests. Consequently, a single urine specimen undergoes numerous changes-of-hand during the testing and confirmation process.

---

[1]Syva Company, Palo Alto, California, literature insert 3M314–17, April 1986, Section 2.
[2]American Management Association Research Study, *Drug Abuse, The Workplace Issues,* AMA Membership Publication, New York, 1987, p. 36.
[3]Ibid., p. 49.

THE GRIEVANCE

On January 2, 1986, employee Fuller[4] reported for drug testing, chosen by her badge number on the computerized random draw. Fuller worked as an initiating explosives operator leader, maintained a good work record, and had never been reported by her supervisor as acting erratically while at work.

Fuller followed sampling procedures, then was informed by the medical department nurse that the sample tested positive for cannabinoids (metabolites of THC) as well as amphetamines. The sample was couriered to Labette County Medical Center (LCMC), then forwarded to National Health Lab (NHL). In a report dated January 6, 1985, the NHL stated that the sample tested was "presumptively positive for cannabinoids. . . . positive by immunoassay only." Fuller was informed of the NHL's results, instructed to undergo a mandatory drug abuse counseling program, and suspended for five days. She was also advised that she would be tested on a regular basis, and if the drug level in her body did not diminish, she would be subject to further disciplinary action.

Fuller returned from suspension on January 23 and was reclassified to an explosives operator at a lower rate of pay due to safety considerations. On February 4, however, Fuller was again reclassified to an explosives operator leader due to a bid upgrade. The following day, Fuller voluntarily submitted to drug screening; there was no evidence of drug metabolites in her sample.

On March 11, Fuller was summoned to take another urine test in the plant medical department. The nurse had difficulty calibrating the machine, ran the test, and informed Fuller that the results were positive for cannabinoids. Fuller adamantly contested the nurse's results. A second nurse was called, and assisted the first nurse in recalibrating the machine and rerunning the test. Again the results were positive. Later that day, Fuller filed a grievance and went to her personal physician to have another urine specimen taken.

On March 21, NHL reported to the company that Fuller's presumed sample tested positive for cannabinoids by immunoassay. Day & Zimmerman terminated Fuller for having tested positive for drugs a second time. On March 22, NHL forwarded a confirming test result from their lab in Virginia, indicating that the Fuller sample tested positive for marijuana by the thin layer chromatography method.

A few days later, Fuller submitted the results of her personal physician's test, also run at NHL. The report stated that there were no drugs in her system. Because of the conflicting results, Day & Zimmerman's

---

[4]The name is fictitious.

industrial relations director reinstated Fuller with back pay as of April 22, 1986. However, she again was reclassified down to explosives operator.

When Fuller reported for work April 22, she was ordered to take another drug test. She gave her urine sample, but did not stay to witness the running of the test. Two nurses in the medical department ran Fuller's specimen three times; all three tests showed positive for drugs. The following morning, one of the nurses hand-carried Fuller's sample to LCMC for forwarding to NHL. In a report dated April 22, NHL reported the sample attributed to Fuller tested positive by immunoassay; a confirming positive report by the GC/Mass Spectometry method was forwarded on May 8, 1986.

On April 22, Fuller was informed that her sample was again positive. Again she protested both the procedure and the results, volunteering to go directly to LCMC for another urine sample. NHL's April 24 report showed positive for marijuana; this was confirmed by a May 14 GC/Mass Spectrometry.

Fuller was discharged on May 13 for testing positive twice under the drug abuse program. The industrial relations director refused Fuller's request to review the drug testing results. Fuller filed a grievance claiming that her discharge was not for just and proper cause, and requesting reinstatement with back pay.

That same month, the AFL-CIO Executive Council announced its "Mandatory Drug and Alcohol Tests" policy, which states in part:

> We deplore the recent efforts by many employers . . . [to] impose punitive programs which ride roughshod over the rights and dignity of the workers and are unnecessary to secure a safe and efficient workforce.
>
> The AFL-CIO urges its affiliates to vigorously resist these harsh and unjustifiable programs and to assist union members who are injured by such employer-imposed programs to invoke their rights under federal and state law.

STATUS OF GRIEVANCE RESOLUTION

Fuller's grievance is in the final stage prior to arbitration. Despite much discussion between Local 5–508 and Day & Zimmerman personnel, the company refuses to reinstate Fuller, claiming that her discharge was warranted under numerous sections of the agreement (see Appendix I, p. 109). Apart from the grievance itself, however, are the parties' conflicting views on the random drug testing program.

Company Position

The company denies that the testing itself violates the labor agreement. While there was no provision in its contract with the Army regarding the program until March 1986, the program implemented in December 1985 was the direct result of an Army request. Moreover, the company claims that the Union and employees join with the company in agreeing that working within a munitions plant while drug-impaired is extremely dangerous.

On the broader issue, Day & Zimmerman supports the army's position on random drug testing, asserting that strictures of the Fourth Amendment regarding "unreasonable search and seizure by the government" apply only to persons or entities working for the government itself (*Burdeau* v. *McDowell*, 256 U.S. 463 (1921); *New Jersey* v. *TLO*, 105 S.Ct. 733 (1985)), and that a private company's random drug testing program cannot be construed as a government act.

The Union

Local 5–508 adamantly disagrees with the company's stand on the testing procedure. The union claims it is an odious invasion of the employee's privacy. Management must, the union argues, prove that such drug testing of an individual is warranted, based upon both suspicion that an employee is using drugs, then next proving that such use deleteriously affects the employee's work performance.

Similar to public employees protected under the Fourth Amendment, union employees covered by a collective bargaining agreements have the right to due process. Numerous cases from both the public sector and private arbitration sustain that such *random* drug testing is impermissible (*MBWE Lodge 16* v. *Burlington Northern*, 802 F.2d 1016, 1 IER Cases 789 (8th Cir. 1986); *AFGE* v. *Weinberger*, 1 IER Cases 1137 (S.D. Ga. 1986); *Lovvorn* v. *City of Chattanooga*, 647 F. Supp. 875, 55 LW 2277, 1 IER Cases 1041 (S.D. Tenn. 1986); *Ward School Bus Mfg. Co.*, 60 LA 1983 (Wagner 1973); *General Portland Cement*, 62 LA 377 (Davidson 1974; *Emhart Mfg. Co.*, 63 LA 1265 (McKone 1974)).

QUESTIONS

1. As assigned representatives of union and management, develop appropriate arguments for or against reinstating Fuller.
2. Decide whether to resolve the grievance or submit to arbitration. What is the basis for your decision?

EXHIBIT 1   Drug Screening and Testing Procedure*

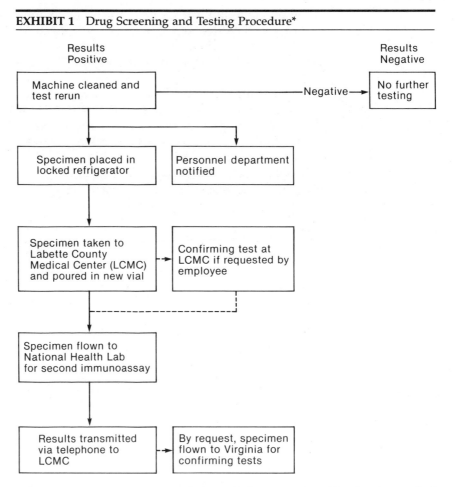

*The immunoassay test measuring drug metabolites is conducted by the plant medical department in employee's presence.

Appendix *Applicable Contract Provisions*

Article III
Management

Section 3.1 The Company shall exercise the usual functions, duties and responsibilities of Management without interference or hindrance by the Union except as abridged by the terms of this Agreement.

Section 3.3 The authority to hire employees, direct, adjust, increase and decrease the working force, to remove employees for just and proper cause and maintain discipline shall be vested in Management, in accordance with the terms of this Agreement.

Article IV
Plant Security and Discipline

Section 4.2 Measures designed to guard against sabotage, espionage, subversive activities and other Plant protective measures which are ordered or approved by the Army representatives shall insofar as practicable be prominently posted throughout the Plant and otherwise made available to employees. Violations of any of these rules or regulations shall be grounds for disciplinary action, including immediate discharge.

Article VII
Arbitration

Section 7.2 The Award of the Arbitrator shall be in writing and shall be final and binding upon the Company, the Union, and the employee or employees involved. The Arbitrator may consider and decide only the particular grievance presented to him and his decision shall be based solely upon an interpretation of the provisions of this Agreement. The Arbitrator shall not have the right to amend, take away, modify, add to, change, or disregard any of the provisions of this Agreement.

Article XII
Safety

Section 12.2 The Union representatives shall assist the Company in enforcing the safety and plant rules and shall inform employees of their liability for failure to obey the safety and plant rules, not only posted rules but all safe practices as determined by the Company. The Company will furnish the Union a copy of the Plant Safety Rules and will discuss the rules with the Union Committee upon request.

Article XIX
Government Contract

Section 19.1 The Company and the Union recognize that the Kansas Army Ammunition Plant is owned by the United States of America and is being operated by the Company under a contract with the United States Army Armament, Munitions and Chemical Command.

Section 19.2 It is the intention of the parties hereto, to enter into an agreement which is in strict conformity with all applicable Federal and State Laws and with the provision of the Prime Contract under which the Contractor is operating this Plant. Should it be determined that any part of this Agreement is contrary to any such laws or any provisions of the Prime Contract, only that portion of this Agreement shall become null and void and the remainder of the Agreement shall remain in full force and effect and the parties will meet to renegotiate the invalid provision so that it will conform to applicable Federal and State laws and the provisions of the Prime Contract.

Ted Porter and the United Brotherhood of Teamsters

Knoxville, advertising itself as "America's Productivity Center," claims only 13.7 percent unionization among its 250,000-person workforce, with Tennessee's Right to Work Laws fully supporting the open-shop philosophy. Other than local plants of national companies, few area manufacturing employers are unionized (see Exhibit 1, p. 117). Preparations for the 1982 World's Fair bolstered local employment, somewhat offsetting the national recessionary trend. As shown in Exhibit 2 (p. 118), however, the postfair year brought a dramatic increase in unemployment as construction and temporary employment waned.

Teamsters Local 519 in Knoxville represents over 2,200 workers in various construction and facility-maintenance trades. Given the cyclical nature of construction-related work, the Teamsters maintain referral contracts with various local employers, some independently and some through the Knoxville Building and Construction Trades Council. As work becomes available, participating employers contact the union hall for referrals. Referred Teamsters are selected from the out-of-work book kept at the union hall. Unemployed Teamsters date and sign the book, to be referred in chronological order as work becomes available. This book is periodically updated and revised.

In January 1980, George Moir was elected Local 519 president. Moir, in turn, appointed Ted Porter as a business agent, whose duties included overseeing the out-of-work book. Porter was released as business agent in September 1981, at which time he signed the out-of-work book.

In 1982, Porter sued Local 519 in state court for allegedly accusing him of theft. Porter was awarded defamation damages of $120,000. Later in 1982, Porter filed charges against the union with the NLRB Regional

---

*This case was based upon a 1985 National Labor Relations Board decision.

Office 10, citing union violations of Section 8(b)(2) and 8(b)(1)(a) of the Act. Region 10's director dismissed the charges in a letter dated February 9, 1983, concluding that there was no evidence to support that (1) the union caused any employer to discriminate against employees; (2) the union failed to refer individuals because they exercised Section 7 rights, or (3) the union referred individuals on the out-of-work list in a discriminatory manner. Porter appealed the regional director's decision, but the general counsel upheld it. In mid-1983, Porter, with others, filed charges against union officers alleging that changes in the by-laws had not been printed as approved by the membership.

Further, Porter's March 1983 work referral to Perini Corporation instigated yet another grievance, and Porter's subsequent December 7, 1983 charge that the union failed in its duty of fair representation (DFR). While the grievance and charge were not one and the same case, the events and resolution of the grievance weighed heavily within Porter's DFR charges against the union.

In March 1983 Porter, along with 14 other union members, was referred to work at the Clinch River Breeder Reactor, for subcontractor Perini Corporation. It was Porter's first referral since signing the out-of-work book in September 1981.

Ten employees were assigned to full-time positions. Porter, a truck driver, along with Teamsters Isbill, Cate, and Branson, were assigned different jobs. Upon reporting for work, the four were often "dogged off" (i.e., immediately sent home). As a result, each only worked about 17 hours the first week. On the evening of March 29, Porter, as spokesperson for the four, approached the area superintendent requesting that the work time be divided up more evenly among the Teamsters. The superintendent retorted heatedly that he "put them where the union hall told him to put them, and that the employees were not running the job."

The following afternoon, employees began gathering at the gate for the 5:00 P.M. shift. Supervisor Cannon pointed at Porter and told him he was laid off, giving him two checks and a layoff slip claiming lack of work. Porter walked over to a truck 20 feet from the gate and sat down.

Cannon then told Isbill, Cate, and Branson that they were dogged off. Isbill, according to Cate, became extremely irate, threatening the supervisors that they would strike the job site. With Isbill still fuming, Isbill and Cate joined Porter at the truck. Porter told Isbill that they'd be fired if they went out on strike. Isbill replied that he didn't give a damn and would put up a line anyway. Porter responded, "Now, Jim, the best thing you can do is go home and forget it and sleep on it."

Later that same evening Porter telephoned Teamsters' business agent Jimmy Metz, requesting that Metz go to the Perini job site and represent him. Metz replied that he wasn't familiar with the applicable contract. According to Porter, he then told Metz that he would contact president

Moir, as some Teamsters wanted to put up a picket line, and if he couldn't get representation, he might as well join them. Metz later stated that Porter told him he had been fired and threatened to put up a picket line and shut the job down.

A few minutes after the Porter-Metz telephone conversation, Moir phoned Porter. Porter asked Moir, too, to go to the job site and represent him. Moir declined to go that night, but indicated that he would call the company in the morning. Porter also told Moir about Isbill's intended picket line, and that if one went up, he'd join in. Moir claimed Porter told him he had been fired and fully intended to strike the job site.

Two days later Porter filed an individual grievance with the union stating that his Perini layoff resulted from his dispute with the superintendent, not lack of work as the layoff slip stipulated. Porter, Isbill, and Cate also filed a joint grievance alleging Perini's unequal work distribution. Both grievances were assigned to Charles L. O'Brien, chairman of the construction division of the Southern Conference of Teamsters.

O'Brien held an April 14 hearing attended by two Perini representatives as well as president Moir. None of the grievants testified at the hearing; Porter was not notified that any hearing was scheduled. Based on Moir's testimony that Porter threatened to strike the job contrary to the no-strike agreement in the contract, O'Brien rejected the grievances.[1]

Porter's layoff papers from Perini indicated a lack of work; after six months without recall, however, Porter surmised that the layoff was permanent, and therefore truly a discharge. On September 27, 1983, Porter filed an 8(a)(3) unfair labor practice against Perini, alleging that he had been discriminatorily discharged on the prior March 30, based on his March 29 dispute with the area superintendent. On December 14, Porter executed a release to Perini in return for a $4,750 payment and withdrew the charge.

The events between March and December 1983, especially the disparity between Porter and the union as to his Perini termination, resulted in disagreement as to the out-of-work book system, and the union's failure to refer Porter following the Perini termination.

HEARING BEFORE THE ADMINISTRATIVE LAW JUDGE

Porter's December 7, 1983 charge alleged that Teamsters Local 519 failed and refused since about June 7 and thereafter to refer Porter for available employment to various employers, including Rust Engineering Com-

---

[1]On March 9, 1984, Porter filed a complaint against the union in the U.S. District Court for the Eastern District of Tennessee, alleging that the union failed to investigate and ineptly handled the case, thus breaching duty of fair representation. The court held that action was barred by the six-month statute of limitations.

pany, with whom the union had a collective bargaining agreement that included an exclusive referral procedure. Such failure and refusal to refer Porter, he asserted, was predicated on his filing charges with the National Labor Relations Board against the union, and on other concerted activities, in violation of Section 8(b)(1)(a) and (2) of the National Labor Relations Act.

Referral System: September 1981–December 1983

Moir and the union trustee contended that a member did not lose his place on the out-of-work book if he was laid off prior to completing 60 days of employment. If a Teamster quit a job prior to the 60 days, however, the union deemed it unfair to force another member to wait even longer. Thus, the member that voluntarily quit must re-sign the out-of-work book in order to be eligible for further referrals. In 1982 the union claimed it adopted a similar policy for discharged employees. Yet if a grievance procedure established that the discharge was illegal or unjust, Moir indicated that this policy could be waived. Porter, believing he was laid-off, never re-signed the book; Moir, claiming Porter was fired, ceased referring him to jobs.

Porter, in fact, claimed that the purported 1982 policy change had never been applied until his termination. Another Teamster, Charlie Lee, was fired by Perini in late November after driving a large dump truck over a car. The out-of-work book contained the notation, "Fired at Perini— 1 day. . . . Stone & Webster 12/19/83." Moir indicated that despite the notation, his investigation of the incident revealed that Perini only claimed Lee was unqualified for driving dump trucks.

Moir's out-of-work book was comprised of some pages listing names single spaced, and others with blank lines in between each name. When Porter had maintained the out-of-work book, each page had been pre-printed and lined. Porter left one line blank for the Teamster's name, then drew rectangles encompassing four additional lines in which to make various notations such as the notation on Lee.

According to Teamster Johnny Black, he approached Moir in early 1983 requesting a referral. Moir looked through the front of the current out-of-work book, and instructed Black to sign in between two other names. Although there were several names listed above his, Black commenced work at Perini within two hours of signing the book. When Black told other union members of the incident, they didn't believe him. Consequently, Black accompanied several other Teamsters to the union hall in April to prove it. Unfortunately, the original book was missing, and the revised version did not contain Black's signature. In yet a later revised version, Black's signature appears on page 29, dated September 29, 1983. Black claimed the signature was a forgery. Moir admitted that when the out-of-work book is periodically revised, union personnel copy names from edition to edition, without requiring that all unemployed Teamsters re-sign the book.

Teamster Cotter's name appeared on page three of the revised out-of-work book, before Porter's September 1981 signing. In mid-July, Cotter was referred to a truck driver position for Rust Engineering Company, also a subcontractor at Clinch River Breeder Reactor. Cotter claimed, however, that he had signed the original book in November 1982. Porter also claimed that another Teamster, James Neal, started work at Rust on July 21, despite Neal's later signing of the book.

As a result of Cotter's and Neal's work referrals, Porter went to the union hall on August 1 to discuss the referrals with Moir. At that time, Moir informed Porter that his name had been moved to the bottom of the list because Perini had fired him. Porter protested, claiming that he had the layoff slip to prove it, but went ahead and re-signed the out-of-work book. While doing so, the union secretary requested that he skip a line, which Porter refused to do.

Despite his re-signing of the book, Porter still was not referred for work. Teamsters Ellis and Davidson, however, signing the book September 15 and November 11 respectively, were referred to Rust Engineering. Moir indicated that both Ellis and Davidson had security clearances as required by Rust since June 1983.[2] Four Teamsters without security clearance, however, had been referred to Rust Engineering after the purported June 1983 policy. Moir contended that these individuals, performing work commensurate with Porter's skills, worked only in nonsecurity areas. Teamster Cate stated that he worked in high security areas, with a guard accompanying him.

Porter questioned the validity of the security clearance requirement, as each clearance cost the company approximately $3,000. Once on the job, the company initiates clearances. For the nature of work being performed, Porter found this highly unlikely. Moir professed no knowledge of clearance procedures.

Referral System: January 1984

Because of numerous questions regarding the out-of-work referral system, the union adopted new referral rules in January 1984. According to Moir, the new system was an index-card type, with each card containing information about the job applicant. Information on the 437 members in the out-of-work book was transferred over to individual cards,

---

[2]Rust provided a letter dated April 9, 1984, stating that this had been their policy at the time in question.

one per person, each numbered according to the order found in the out-of-work book. Individuals were not allowed to see the actual cards, as Moir claimed he did not "have the time to take up with them coming in and harassing [him]."

Rules for the new system read:

> All persons desiring to be referred from the hiring hall shall personally provide the President and the Business Manager with their name, address, telephone number, industry to which referral is desired, and shall also provide such other information as is necessary to determine their length of time or service in the industry, places of employment and qualifications for work in the industry to which referral is desired.
>
> No person shall be allowed to register for referral unless they are currently unemployed. A person shall be considered unemployed when not working or when working on a job of short duration which shall be defined as ten (10) days or less. Any persons registering for referral from the hiring hall shall renew their registration the first of every month.
>
> The President and Business Manager shall make referrals to those employers requesting workers from among the persons who have registered for referral, taking into consideration the information provided by the persons upon registration.

The rules were posted at the union hall, and mailed to stewards for posting at work locations.

The same month, Moir held a general membership meeting attended by 50 Teamsters during which he explained the new rules. Moir explained that monthly renewal entailed a member coming to the union hall and initialing and dating the back of the card. This rule was waived for persons living 50 or 60 miles away, who could telephone the union, informing them of their availability for work. This exception, however, was not in the promulgated rules.

Several union members encountered difficulty with the new system. Porter attended the general membership meeting; he was hesitant to sign the card. However, he went to the union hall monthly to inform them that he was available for work. Burgess also attended the meeting, and the union secretary filled out the card without requesting his signature. Later, while paying monthly dues to the secretary, she never requested that he initial the card. Cate did not recall that the card had to be signed or initialed. The union secretary filled out Isbill's card, but Isbill declined to sign it. The secretary said, "You're number 62; remember that number." Later, however, she told Isbill that he was number 82. Isbill also did not know that he was supposed to initial the card monthly, although he did go to the union hall monthly to inform them of his availability for work.

Moir waited two months for the word of the new system to circulate among Teamsters. After that, he eliminated approximately 200 individuals from the referral system for failure to come in and renew their status, including Porter and Isbill.

Union's Brief

In its brief to the administrative law judge, the union's counsel argued for several legal technicalities:

1. Porter cannot litigate the Perini discharge or the union's disposition of the grievance in this proceeding as barred by Section 10(b) six-month statute of limitations.

2. That Porter is estopped from proceedings in this matter by the regional director's dismissal of DFR charges, filed by Porter in late 1982, in that many of the same legal issues and facts that are common to the current complaint were reviewed earlier.

3. That the board should require Porter to utilize the appeals mechanism within the union's new rules before taking action on his unfair labor practice charge, as doing so encourages quick and peaceful resolutions of labor disputes.

TASK

As assigned union or Porter advocates, prepare your arguments for the administrative law judge hearing.

EXHIBIT 1 Knoxville Area Manufacturing Employers

Firm	Employees	Union Affiliation
Standard Knitting	2,000	None
Levi Strauss	1,949	UGW
Robertshaw Controls	1,400	USW-IAM
Palm Beach	800	ACTWU
BIKE Athletic	600	ACTWU
ASARCO	541	ICW
Kern's Inc.	450	None
Normak International	400	None
Sea Ray Boats	400	None
TRW, Carr Division	395	OCAW
Alpha Industries	380	None
London Fog	375	ACTWU
Lay Packing	350	None
Tom's Foods	250	None
Volunteer Apparel	220	None

EXHIBIT 2   Knoxville Employment Data

Industry	MSA* INDUSTRY	
	Percent Employment	Average Weekly Wages
Manufacturing	22.0%	$380
Construction	4.5	300
Transportation, communication, and utilities	3.5	400
Trade	25.0	220
Finance, insurance, and real estate	3.5	320
Services	21.0	295
Government	20.0	290
Other	0.5	—

	SMSA† LABOR FORCE DATA			
	1980	1981	1982	1983
Total labor force	217,400	228,600	233,900	231,100
Unemployment rate	6.0%	7.6%	8.9%	10.5%

*MSA = Metropolitan Statistical Area (Anderson, Blount, Grainger, Jefferson, Knox, Sevier, and Union counties, accounting for approximately 40,000 more workers than the SMSA).

† SMSA = Standard MSA (Anderson, Blount, Knox, and Union counties).

Labor Relations in Transition

Steel Industry Background Note

INDUSTRY BACKGROUND

Although perhaps not quite mom and apple pie, the domestic steel industry forms an integral part of American heritage. A young Scottish immigrant, Andrew Carnegie, entered the iron and steel business in 1865. Carnegie eventually amassed his manufacturing interests into Carnegie Steel in 1899, merged with U.S. Steel in 1901, and retired to a world of philanthropy. U.S. Steel, applying Carnegie's business ideology that all innovation be internally funded, remained the unrivaled world steel producer for more than half of the 20th century. Other domestic steel producers patterned themselves after U.S. Steel. As the industry matured, profits tightened, and the U.S. steel industry fell behind in modernization.

Steel Production

Steel comes in two generic product categories: carbon steel, accounting for 85 percent of sales, and specialty steels, accounting for the remaining 15 percent of steel products sold. Exhibit 1 (p. 132) lists steel sales by product type. Carbon steels contain very small amounts of the alloying elements manganese, silicon, and copper. Due to ease of forming and welding, carbon steel is used primarily for flat-rolled products, such as the production of machines, auto bodies, buildings, and ship hulls.

There are three types of specialty steels: alloy, stainless, and high-strength, low-alloy (HSLA). Alloy steels contain specific percentages of vanadium, molybdenum, or other alloys, as well as larger amounts of manganese, silicon, and copper than carbon steel. Utilized where greater strength, corrosion-resistance, and electrical attributes are required, alloy steels account for 13 percent of industry volume. Stainless steel, most of which is chromium nickel steel, accounts for less than 2 percent of industry volume. Because of stainless steel's high rust and corrosion resistance, it is used primarily in aerospace, medical, and petrochemical industries. The newest alloy, high-strength, low-alloy steel (HSLA), contains smaller amounts of alloying elements, yet gains strength through special processing. Early markets include automobiles, railroad freight cars, and commercial buildings, where strength and weight are important. Exhibit 2 (p. 133) summarizes the major steel customers for all products and changes in customer demand from 1980–86.

Steel, whether carbon or specialty, is produced in either integrated or nonintegrated steel mills. These types of facilities vary according to technological leadership and labor efficiency. Technical obsolescence mainly affects domestic integrated steel mills; since the mid-50s, only two new integrated U.S. steel-making facilities have been built. Most nonintegrated facilities were built after 1960, incorporating modern production techniques.

Approximately 30 integrated steel mills, with blast furnaces, coke ovens, as well as steelmaking facilities, supply 80 percent of domestic production. Integrated operations are composed of six primary steps: coke production (for use in the blast furnace); pelletizing or sintering iron ore; ironmaking in the blast furnace (which reduces iron ore to metallic iron); refining pig iron and addition of alloying elements (utilizing either an open hearth, basic oxygen, or electric arc process); casting (either ingot or continuous); and finishing via various mechanical rolling procedures. Exhibits 3a and 3b (pp. 133–134) provide a schematic of traditional integrated steel production. Not surprisingly, integrated mills are highly capital intensive, averaging net plant values of over $37,000 per employee. Integrated mills sell a variety of products worldwide.

Most steel mills in the United States are nonintegrated, although each mill has a much smaller annual output than the integrated mills. Nonintegrated mills comprise just 20 percent of domestic production. Nonintegrated mills skip the coking, pelletizing, and ironmaking processes, utilizing steel scrap as the primary input. Consequently, their net plant value averages only $20,000 per employee whether the mill produces specialty or carbon steel. Nonintegrated specialty steel producers market their products worldwide, whereas nonintegrated carbon steel facilities utilizing scrap-based electric arc furnaces (minimills) service local markets with a narrow product range.

Technological Innovation

Steelmaking innovation centers around two key factors: increasing energy efficiency and reducing handling costs. Referring again to Exhibits 3a and 3b, innovations within and between these various steps will be discussed.

Refining the Melt. Open hearth furnace (HF) technology evolved at the turn of the century. Scrap, limestone, and iron ore are melted by flames in a shallow open hearth bed, to which molten pig iron is added. Hot fuel gases are then ignited and passed over the surface of the molten metal. While versatile in that the scrap-to-hot-metal ratio can vary according to availability and materials prices, the OHF process requires five to eight hours to produce output. As a result, its use has steadily declined since the mid-60s, being replaced by the basic oxygen furnace (BOF) and electric arc furnace (EAF). OHF production now accounts for less than 8 percent of total domestic steel production.

The basic oxygen furnace (BOF) technology, developed after World War II, gained popularity only after bulk oxygen production became feasible. In the BOF process, a supersonic stream of oxygen is directed through a closed-bottom, pear-shaped vessel containing scrap, pig iron, and slag formers. After refinement, the molten steel is poured into ladles where alloying elements are added. The process takes between 35 and 45 minutes to complete. BOF technology accounts for almost 60 percent of domestic steel production.

Electric arc furnace technology was developed during the 60s, and originally only used in specialty steel production because it is a far more controllable process than either OHF or BOF. Another advantage is that EAFs use 100 percent cold scrap, and scrap prices tend to be substantially lower than pig iron prices. After loading the furnace with cold scrap, graphite electrodes are lowered, and a charge passes between them, over the scrap, melting the batch. Another benefit of EAFs is their lower initial investment cost, approximately one third per ton of annual output than either OHF or BOF. Currently accounting for over 30 percent of domestic steel production, the EAF's inherent growth limits are the availability and price of scrap steel.

Ladle Technology. After heating and prior to casting, a melt travels in ladles, where various alloying elements are added. Recently, however, more and more steel companies utilize this process step to further refine the melt, yielding higher quality steel. Induction stirring, argon stirring, vacuum degassing, and particle injection are a few ladle techniques that improve steel quality.

Casting and Finishing. As depicted in Exhibit 3a, raw steel historically was poured into large ingot molds. After solidifying, ingots were cropped, reheated, and hot-rolled into blooms, billets, or slabs. Continuous (strand) casting evolved to realize the energy and cost savings of foregoing the ingot-making step. In continuous casting, molten steel pours into a water-cooled mold corresponding to the desired semifinished shape. Water-sprayed, the shape solidifies, then is roller-straightened and cut to size. Not only does continuous casting save the molding-reheating step, it also produces 10 percent greater product yield.

Following casting, blooms are reheated and finished into structural shapes and rails; billets are rolled into bars, wire, or pipe; and slabs are formed into either hot- or cold-rolled sheet, and strip or plates. Continuous casting into these finished shapes results in higher product yields and lower labor costs. However, direct continuous casting is extremely expensive, and its widespread use may not be economically feasible. One solution to this problem is generic steel production. Economies of scale are achieved by consolidating steel grades, producing more of fewer steel types. One domestic producer moving toward generic grades is U.S. Steel division of USX. Borrowing technology from Nippon Kokan and Daido Steel, U.S. Steel implemented generic steel production in its Gary Works in 1986.

General Process Control. Because of the production complexity, steel producers increasingly use computer software to increase efficiency throughout the process. Optimizing algorithms determine stock selection, roll schedules, and material allotment. Other programs monitor and regulate gas and other energy inputs, controlling fuel costs.

International Strategies: Survival in Decline

Worldwide steel demand flattened shortly after World War II while worldwide production capacity continued to grow. Despite this, the U.S. supplied almost half of the world's steel in 1950 out of the integrated facilities built earlier in the century. The 50s and 60s, however, marked a modernization period for many non-U.S. steel producers, with U.S. facilities becoming more and more obsolete and cost inefficient. Over half the steel produced in West Germany, France, and the United Kingdom comes from plants either modernized or built since the 50s. All Japanese steel facilities are new. By contrast, only about 10 percent of current U.S. output comes from plants less than 33 years old, with U.S. producers now holding less than one fifth of the worldwide market share.

Another trend affecting the domestic industry's competitive position is the nationalization of many steel industries outside the United States. While the governments of Canada and the United States have intervened during labor negotiations, governments in such countries as Belgium, France, and the United Kingdom have either participated in or taken control of their domestic steel industry. Capital for new steelmaking facilities in developing countries, where most capacity growth is anticipated, can only be generated by government loans or grants. Thus, industry nationalization is expected to increase through the end of the century.

Increasing nationalization results in two competitive disadvantages for U.S. producers. First, government subsidization exacerbates the U.S.

producers' already technologically noncompetitive cost position in a price-sensitive market (see Exhibit 4, p. 134). This cost differential leaves the shrinking domestic market vulnerable to import penetration. Second, many non-U.S. producers maintain local pricing policies or high import tariffs that restrict the United States' export market. As illustrated in Exhibit 5 (see p. 135), the net result of these two circumstances is increasing import penetration at home and decreasing exportation abroad. The net of this net, as it were, is steadily declining steel capacity, production, and contribution to the U.S. economy (see Exhibit 6, p. 135).

U.S. Trade Restrictions

One response to the worldwide nationalization of the industry is to impose U.S. trade restrictions. While trade restrictions come in a variety of packages, from voluntary restraint agreements such as used on Japanese automobiles until the early 80s, to trigger price mechanisms, to adjustment assistance, two key trade restrictions applying to the domestic steel industry have been countervailing and antidumping restrictions. Both of these restrictions provide for import duties in an effort to equalize import and domestic prices. Applying these restrictions is a two-step process.

The International Trade Administration of the U.S. Department of Commerce determines whether a country directly or indirectly provides subsidization of manufacturing, production, or exportation of product imported into the United States (initiating countervailing restrictions); or whether foreign products are being sold in the United States for less than their fair market value (initiating antidumping restrictions). In either case, the International Trade Commission must then determine whether "an industry in the United States is materially injured, or is threatened with material injury, or the establishment of an industry in the United States is materially retarded, by reasons of imports of that merchandise."[1] If so determined, a duty is imposed equal to the amount of the net subsidy (countervailing duty) or value differential (antidumping duty).

Domestic Response to Declining Demand

While alleviating import versus domestic price disparities, trade restrictions have not abated declining demand. Suffering from marked overcapacity in outdated facilities, domestic steel producers have responded with partial or full plant closures, facility modernization, diversification into other product lines, and company reorganization.

---

[1]Trade Agreements Act of 1979, Section 701(a) and 731(a)(b).

Integrated steel mills are not readily converted into other manufacturing facilities; buyers seldom offer more than the net value of the assets. Consequently, plants are simply closed, assets sold, and losses reported on the companies' financial statements. Between 1974 and 1984, 475 domestic plants were closed due to excess capacity.

Despite reported paper losses, which occur against book value, plant closures and subsequent asset sales usually generate real cash. For example, Inland Steel, trimming the company to only one steelmaking operation, utilized the resulting cash flow to completely modernize that one facility. Kaiser Steel Corporation shut down most of their steelmaking operations, attracting numerous takeover bids in light of their coal and cash reserves.

Closure-generated cash reserves also enable steel companies to diversify into growth, nonsteel industries. In 1981 U.S. Steel, the historical steelmaking leader, purchased Marathon Oil. As a result, steel's contribution to company revenues is less than half the 1979 level, with U.S. Steel's steel revenues now raking ninth in the nation (see Exhibit 7, p. 136). National Intergroup announced diversification plans with the proposed 1984 Bergen Brunswig Corporation merger. The proposed merger with the drug distributor would have greatly reduced National Intergroup's reliance on steel revenues. Following a proxy fight between the company and a large institutional investor, stockholders approved the merger in early 1985. However, Bergen called off the merger, citing National's worsening metals business as the reason. Later that year, National Intergroup acquired a smaller nonsteel company.

Companies throughout the industry are also reorganizing their organizational structures. U.S. Steel reduced white-collar employment by over 50 percent; Bethlehem Steel eliminated white-collar jobs and cut salaries of those who remained. Still other steel companies are reorganizing under the protection of Chapter 11 bankruptcy proceedings.

Chapter 11 can provide competitive cost advantages to firms seeking its protection, allowing complete reorganization without liability. For example, labor contracts, pension fund liabilities, and personal injury claims can all be abrogated under Chapter 11 despite the 1984 congressional amendments aimed at reducing such misuse of federal bankruptcy proceedings. Such a determination is still at the discretion of bankruptcy judges. The federal Pension Benefit Guaranty Corporation picked up over $642 million in unfunded pension liabilities following Wisconsin Steel, McLouth Steel, Phoenix Steel Corporation, and Wheeling-Pittsburgh Chapter 11 reorganizations. LTV Corporation's 1986 filing added another possible $1.5 billion in unfunded pension liabilities to that total.

A bankruptcy judge's ruling may also allow significant labor cost savings. Wheeling-Pittsburgh, unable to gain concessions during 1985 contract negotiations, filed for Chapter 11. Four days after the bankruptcy judge ruled the labor contract void, over 8,000 steelworkers walked out. Three months later, workers returned to $18 per hour wages (a 16 percent decrease) while the rest of the industry negotiated wages of around $22 per hour.

Employment Impact

While steel companies streamline operations, the brunt of such activity is borne by the work force. Over a quarter of a million steel industry hourly jobs have been lost since 1979, and 105,000 white-collar steel industry jobs have been permanently eliminated. Such displacement not only threatens the livelihood of workers, but also greatly affects the 300 steel communities nationwide, such as in the Mon Valley, south of Pittsburgh, where the suicide rate is about twice the national average.

In addition to permanent layoffs resulting from plant closures, plant modernization also affects workers, both in numbers and required skill level. An example of this is the shift from open hearth furnaces to basic oxygen furnaces. Open hearth furnaces require a great number of unskilled workers, whereas basic oxygen furnaces require fewer, but more skilled workers. Finally, workers remaining on the job face lower wages as concessions and givebacks increase within industry negotiations.

LABOR BACKGROUND

History

The steel industry boasts the oldest industrial union on record, the Sons of Vulcan, secretly organized in 1858. By 1876, the Sons of Vulcan merged with other unions, forming the Amalgamated Association of Iron, Steel, and Tin Workers of North America. By the turn of the century, the Amalgamated had lost much worker support following numerous defeated strike efforts against the major steel companies. By the mid-30s, the Amalgamated represented only 10 percent of all steel workers.

In May 1937, the CIO and John Lewis, president of the United Mine Workers (UMW), formed the Steelworkers Organizing Committee (SWOC), chaired by former UMW vice president Philip Murray. Organizing U.S. Steel's 220,000 workers in 1937 was a major victory for SWOC. "Little Steel," however, comprised of Bethlehem, Inland, Republic, Youngstown Sheet and Tube, American Rolling Mill, and National Steel, resisted organization attempts despite some of the most bitter and violent strikes in U.S. history. In 1941, SWOC finally won representation at all Bethlehem plants; shortly thereafter, the balance of Little Steel signed contracts. By 1942, when the Amalgamated merged with the

SWOC to form the United Steelworkers of America, the group represented 660,000 workers, 63 percent of steel industry hourly employees.

While garnering support of individual workers, the USWA functioned as a highly centralized, autocratic union with a specific goal: to eliminate wage inequities within and across companies, thereby removing wages from competition. To accomplish this goal against the mighty steel conglomerates, the union needed the power to shut down the entire industry. According to President Murray, this power remained vested at the national union level, with local unions having little autonomy. Until his death in 1953, Murray also exerted considerable influence over the executive board, consisting of the national officers, the national director of Canada, and 25 district directors. David McDonald, also a former UMW, succeeded Murray. In 1957, the autocracy of the union was challenged when Donald Rarick, leader of a dues protest movement, garnered 35 percent of the vote. Over the next 30 years, local member involvement would continue to be a key campaign issue.

In 1965, I. W. Abel was elected president, the first steelworker to achieve that position, on a platform stressing local issues. Emil Narik challenged Abel in 1969 in a close race. Narik's defeat resulted in a challenged election and revelation of glaring faults within the union's electoral procedures. In 1977, due to Abel's mandatory retirement, two non-incumbents competed for the first time. Lloyd McBride, pro-Abel, won narrowly, despite Edward Sadlowski's platform that union leadership worked too closely with industry management to the detriment of local issues. Also, for the first time, a Canadian—Lynn Williams— was elected to a national officer position.

McBride's first move as president was to reorganize the National. Pushing day-to-day administration down to the vice-presidential level, McBride charged the presidency with overseeing the increasing legal and legislative issues.

Bargaining Structure

Historically, rank-and-file input into negotiation issues existed via the Wage Policy Committee. The Wage Policy Committee is comprised of the executive board and 145 elected district delegates. The committee is charged with setting bargaining policy based on resolution of local, district, and international convention issues. Until the industry conferences were established in 1966, the committee also recommended strikes and contract ratification or rejection.

Each of the 19 industry conferences is restricted to members directly affected by negotiations within an industry. Comprised of local union members plus district directors and presiding officers as designated by the international president, each local has a single vote in a conference, regardless of membership size. Only the four conferences within industrywide bargaining (basic steel, aluminum, nonferrous metals, and containers) have authority to draw up bargaining proposals for companies within their industry. These four recommend strikes to the executive board and determine contract settlements. While strikes must be supported by industry membership vote, no such vote is necessary in determining contract resolution. The remaining 15 conferences, characterized by single-plant or single-employer bargaining, operate under the Wage Policy Committee's general collective bargaining goals.

The framework of company-by-company agreements within an industrywide bargaining structure evolved over time. In the early years, most companies followed the U.S. Steel settlement. In 1955, however, six companies agreed to negotiate at the union's headquarters in Pittsburgh rather than at their various headquarters throughout the East and Midwest. While each company committee negotiated separately with the union, the decision represented consolidation of negotiation sites. In 1956, 12 companies delegated a single four-member committee to negotiate major issues. In 1959, committee jurisdiction extended to include all negotiation issues, not just the major ones. It is speculated that the companies elected this industrywide bargaining format in an effort to combat the union solidarity. Also, as the union had eliminated wage and benefit differentials between companies, little would be gained by individual bargaining. Moreover, such a move minimized selective strike activity; the Taft-Hartley Act minimized chances of industrywide strikes.

Following a 1959 strike, the union and industry acknowledged the need for an ongoing problem-solving relationship on negotiation issues. The following year the parties activated the Human Relations Research Committee agreed to in the 1959 contract, facilitating continuous discussion on wages, benefits, job classifications and seniority. Yet to the membership, this method for early resolution of negotiation issues meant a bad settlement. Mid-60s negotiations dissolved the committee, leaving only provisions for joint study of apprenticeship training, testing, and grievance and arbitration procedures within the contract.

Negotiation History

Strikes have been part and parcel to steel industry negotiations since the late 1800s. While often violent, most early strikes were ineffective, with workers returning to lesser packages than first offered by the companies. However, the Great Depression, the National Industry Recovery Act of 1933, the National Labor Relations Act, and the 1935 formation of the SWOC breathed new life into the union movement. While the turbulent 1937 Little Steel strikes appeared fruitless, unfair labor practice charges against the companies eventually won workers millions of dollars in back pay; the 1941 NLRB-ordered rerun elections brought the union into Little Steel.

The War Labor Board averted major strikes during World War II. In contract negotiations following the war, government still played a vital mediation role. The 750,000-worker 1946 strike was resolved via three-way negotiations between the union, the industry, and the government, with the union gaining wage increases only after the government allowed the steel companies to raise prices. In 1951–52, deadlocked negotiations reconvened in front of the Wage Stabilization Board. The Board's recommended wage increases, increases in fringe benefits, and union shop clause were rejected by the steel companies. To circumvent a strike during the Korean War, President Truman seized the steel industry on April 8, 1952, under the inherent powers of the presidency. On June 2, the Supreme Court ruled the president's actions unconstitutional; hours later, 560,000 steelworkers went out on a strike that lasted 59 days, creating catastrophic conditions within the war mobilization effort. A compromise agreement was reached in the White House in late July.

The 1959 strike heralded both the onslaught of foreign competition, and a new era of relative labor peace. The union wanted new provisions for job security; companies sought to eliminate local working conditions clauses. The ensuing strike shut down 87 percent of the industry for 116 days. President Eisenhower invoked the national emergency disputes provisions of the Taft-Hartley Act. The secretary of labor and the vice president of the United States worked with the parties to reach an agreement. However, for the first time in history, steel imports exceeded U.S. steel exports. The trend never reversed.

Three decades of hostile negotiations left their mark on the industry. Despite labor peace during the 60s, steel customers invariably stockpiled product, hedging against historical strike activity. Following a settlement, production waned as inventories slowly depleted. More and more customers relied on offshore steel producers to bypass domestic labor squabbles altogether.

In an effort to ameliorate the industry's reputation, USWA President Abel recommended in 1967 that the union formally forsake "crisis bargaining." Abel suggested that unresolved negotiation issues be subject to binding interest arbitration, not strike activity. While his initial program was defeated, he resurrected a variation, the Experimental Negotiating Agreement (ENA), in 1973. The membership accepted ENA with the following stipulations:

1. Local unions maintained the right to strike over local issues.
2. Each steel employee received a $150 bonus.
3. Guaranteed minimum wage increase of 3 percent per year.
4. Guaranteed minimum cost-of-living increases tied to the consumer price index.

5. Arbitration decisions would not affect local working conditions, union shop and checkoff provisions, management rights, or the four stipulations cited above.

While ENA appeared successful for 1970s negotiations, it was doomed following the 1982 recession. Steel industry unemployment was 40 percent; plants still operating averaged 46 percent capacity utilization. U.S. Steel had diversified out of steel the year before with the purchase of Marathon Oil; three other steel companies were destined for Chapter 11. Major steel producers claimed that the ENA membership provisions were too costly a quid pro quo for averted strikes. USW President McBride finally negotiated a concession package which included wage reductions, staffing eliminations, and permitted local unions to negotiate craft consolidation in exchange for unionized plant construction.

While 1983 concessions reduced labor costs to 33 percent of total costs, Wheeling-Pittsburgh demanded more. The union declined the company's last offer, Wheeling-Pittsburgh filed Chapter 11, and the bankruptcy judge abrogated the labor contract. In the largest strike since 1959, 8,000 workers walked out. The company and union remained at odds until Wheeling-Pittsburgh appointed a new chairman who allowed two union representatives on the board of directors. Negotiated wages were significantly reduced below other steel companies.

In 1986 USX (formerly U.S. Steel) faced a union embittered by USX's diversification, offshore partnerships, and 23,000 layoffs during the first six months of that year. When the contract expired August 1, 1986, 22,000 workers covering 25 plants in nine states conducted the longest steel strike in American history. After the six-month strike, workers returned to reduced wages and less restrictive work rules in exchange for limited subcontracting, profit sharing, and capital investment in two domestic facilities. The strike resulted in USX reporting a 1986 fourth-quarter loss of $1.42 billion, the largest in the company's history, and one of the largest losses in U.S. corporate history.

Cooperation in Conflict

Steel industry and labor history combined to form a unique labor-management relationship, one constantly poised between cooperation and fierce conflict. Labor's strength allowed for numerous provisions and wage packages far ahead of general manufacturing. The industry's maturity, reached shortly after World War II, encouraged the parties to cooperate on key issues facing the industry despite negotiation conflict.

The parties' first cooperative venture did much to ensure steelworkers' long-term economic gain. In January 1947, the joint Cooperative Wage Study agreement eliminated intra- as well as interplant inequities among 180,000 jobs in 450 basic steel plants. The initial framework provided for 30 job classifications with a fixed 3.5-cent wage differential between classifications. This framework ensured commensurately higher earnings for higher job classifications compared with flatly applied percentage increases.

In 1956 workers gained cost-of-living allowance (COLA) contract provisions, calculated as a fixed dollar amount tied to increases in the consumer price index. As a result of the job classification system and COLA provisions, in 1977 steelworkers earned, on average, one-and-a-half times the hourly rate of other manufacturing; steel production worker output per man hour, on the other hand, was slightly less.

Other unique contract gains included limited subcontracting provisions (1963) and the specificity of local working conditions despite industrywide bargaining.

While conflict gained better packages for steelworkers, the industry-union relationship was also hallmarked by cooperative ventures. The Cooperative Wage Study was followed by the Human Relations Research Committee (1960), the Experimental Negotiating Agreement (1973), the Joint Steel Industry-Union Contracting Out Review Commission (1977–79), and the 1980 contract addition of Appendix 15, the Labor-Management Participation Teams Experimental Agreement. Appendix 15 established a work-team framework, the goals of which were to improve product quality, increase worker involvement, and enhance the workplace environment. In 1983, the word *Experimental* was dropped from Appendix 15; by 1985, some 500 labor-management participation teams were functioning within 23 basic steel plants throughout the industry, increasing worker productivity at those sites by an estimated 38 percent.

EXHIBIT 1   Steel Product Shipments as Percent of Total U.S. Steel Shipments, 1980–1986

Products	1980	1981	1982	1983	1984	1985	1986
Semifinished steel	6%	6%	6%	6%	6%	6%	7%
Structural	6	6	6	5	6	6	7
Plates	10	9	7	6	6	6	5
Rails/access.	2	2	1	1	2	1	1
Bars/tool steel	16	16	18	17	18	17	17
Pipe/tubing	11	12	8	5	6	6	4
Wire products	2	2	2	2	2	2	2
Tin mill products	7	6	6	6	6	5	5
Sheets	38	40	43	49	47	48	49
Strip	2	2	2	3	3	2	2
Total shipments*	83.9	87.0	61.6	67.6	73.7	73.0	69.9

* Net tons (000,000 omitted).

Source: American Iron & Steel Institute.

EXHIBIT 2 Changes in Steel Customer Demand, 1980–1986

Customer	Percent of Demand 80	Percent of Change						
		79–80	80–81	81–82	82–83	83–84	84–85	85–86
Automotive	14	−34.9	+ 8.5	−29.4	+32.6	+ 4.6	+ 6.3	− 8.7
Construction	14	−13.4	− 1.8	−26.6	+16.4	+ 1.8	−11.4	− 4.8
Containers	7	−18.0	− 4.7	−15.5	+ 1.4	− 4.0	− 5.2	+ 1.3
Railroads	4	−23.3	−31.5	−52.8	− 8.1	+53.5	−23.5	−23.5
Energy/mining	6	+43.6	+16.1	−56.0	−52.8	+54.6	−10.1	−55.7
Machinery	9	−20.8	+ 3.4	−36.5	+ 5.1	+ 8.9	−23.8	+13.2
Processing	5	−18.6	+22.9	−36.3	+36.7	+16.6	− 4.6	− 3.2
Agriculture	2	−37.1	− 0.9	−23.2	−26.0	− 3.7	−46.5	− 1.2
Shipbuilding	1	+30.0	− 8.3	−63.8	+18.0	0.0	−36.3	−26.3
Warehouses	19	−11.4	+ 9.1	−25.9	+27.9	+ 9.9	+ 0.7	− 5.6
All other	16	−17.4	+18.0	−22.0	−13.0	+16.1	+ 0.7	+ 4.8
Exports	3	+29.3	−28.9	−54.9	−34.6	+78.7	+15.4	+ 0.3
	100%							
Total shipments		−16.4	+ 5.5	−30.4	+ 9.8	+ 9.1	− 1.5	− 4.2

Source: American Iron and Steel Institute.

EXHIBIT 3a Integrated Steel Mill Operation (part 1)

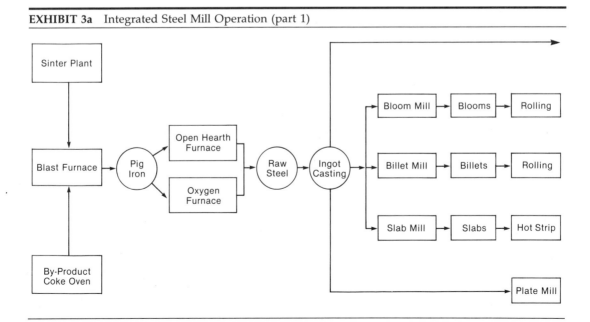

EXHIBIT 3b   Integrated Steel Mill Operation (part 2)

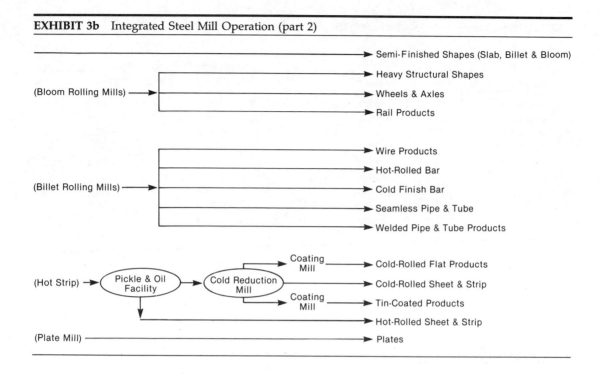

EXHIBIT 4   Relative Worldwide Production Costs (at 90 percent capacity utilization)

Cost	United States	United Kingdom	France	Japan	West Germany
Direct labor*	30%	25%	32%	18%	31%
Materials*	50%	78%	64%	62%	66%
Total cost[†]	116	99	93	82	86

* As percent of total cost.
[†] Indexed: $500/ton = 100.

Source: Office of Technology Assessment

EXHIBIT 5   Percent Import/Export of Steel Mill Products by Group, 1980–1986

Products	1980	1981	1982	1983	1984	1985	1986
Imports							
Semifinished steel	1%	4%	4%	5%	6%	10%	9%
Wire rods	5	5	6	7	6	6	7
Structural	12	10	10	9	8	9	9
Plates	13	12	10	7	6	6	5
Rails/access.	3	2	2	1	1	2	1
Bars/tool steel	6	5	5	6	7	6	7
Pipe/tubing	24	33	32	17	21	18	14
Wire products	5	4	4	5	5	4	5
Tin mill product	2	2	2	3	3	3	3
Sheets and strip	29	24	27	41	38	36	38
Total shipments*	15.5	19.9	16.6	17.0	26.1	24.3	20.7
Exports							
Semifinished steel	22%	19%	20%	9%	8%	10%	6%
Wire rods	5	4	1	.5	1	1	1
Structural	4	5	4	4	3	5	4
Plates	5	7	7	9	9	9	8
Rails/access.	3	3	2	2	2	1	1
Bars/tool steel	11	12	12	14	14	11	9
Pipe/tubing	12	16	23	22	21	21	13
Wire products	1	2	2	2	3	3	4
Tin mill product	22	16	17	21	17	18	30
Sheets and strip	16	17	13	18	23	23	25
Total shipments*	4.1	2.9	1.8	1.2	1.0	.93	.93

* Net tons (000,000 omitted).

Source: American Iron and Steel Institute.

EXHIBIT 6   U.S. Steel Consumption versus Gross National Product, 1980–1986

Year	Domestic Steel Capacity*	Steel Production*	Steel Consumption/GNP
1980	157	110	29.9
1981	157	120	32.5
1982	157	74	24.1
1983	151	81	25.5
1984	135	89	28.3
1985	134	84	24.2
1986	128	80	24.5

* Millions of net tons.

Source: American Iron and Steel Institute; Department of Commerce.

EXHIBIT 7   1986 Rankings of U.S. Steel Companies

Company	Revenues	Profitability ROR*	ROE†
National Intergroup	1	2	5
Interlake	2	1	3
Inland Steel	3	4	6
Wheeling-Pittsburgh	4	8	9
Bethlehem Steel	5	5	7
LTV Corporation	6	9	1
NVF Company	7	6	2
Armco	8	7	8
USX	9	3	4

* ROR = Return on revenues.
† ROE = Return on equity.

Inland Container and the United Steelworkers of America

Throughout the 60s, three domestic steel companies dominated the steel container market. During the 70s, however, 27 new companies entered and competed for the shrinking market, initiating intense price wars. Substitute plastics products and reconditioned steel containers became more and more popular. Customers became more quality conscious, rejecting steel container shipments for poor painting, rust, leakage, or other flaws. Additionally, in the early 1980s, government regulations mandated that traditional steel containers be double lined.

In 1982, Inland Container, a division of Inland Steel Corporation, announced plans to close their New Orleans container production facility, which had been operating at a net loss due to production inefficiencies, layout bottlenecks, and high labor costs. Subsequently, in September, Inland signed an option contract for the right of first refusal for property adjacent to their Canton, Mississippi, pail facility. On December 20, Inland exercised the option.

On May 17, 1983, Local 2179 of the United Steelworkers of America, representing New Orleans workers, filed unfair labor practice charges against Inland Container, charging that Inland Container violated Section 8(d) of the Act by announcing its intent to relocate bargaining unit work to reduce labor costs without first engaging in mandatory bargaining with the union about the decision. Independent of this allegation, the union further asserted that Inland Container violated Section 8(a)(3) by refusing to employ any New Orleans union members at the new Canton facility.

---

*This case was based in part on a June 1985 National Labor Relations Board decision.

INLAND CONTAINER DIVISION

Inland Container division was one of Inland Steel Corporation's five business operations (see Exhibits 1 and 2 p. 143). Inland Container produced steel shipping containers in both pail and drum sizes for industrial customers. The New Orleans and Canton, Mississippi facilities produced steel containers and pails, respectively, for the South. Of Inland's four other plants, two were consolidated container and pail facilities.

Container Products Sales by Group

	1982	1981
Drums	54%	54%
Pails	38	38
Intermediates	4	4
Stainless steel	1	1
Other	3	3

Overall 1982 drum sales earnings were affected by depressed business cycles in petroleum, basic chemical, and coatings industries, the primary drum customers. Pails, while less sensitive to economic downturns, faced increasing competition from plastic products. In response, Inland sought to reduce both fixed and variable costs, including reducing salaried personnel and salary levels.

THE NEW ORLEANS PLANT

Bound on all sides by city streets, the New Orleans container plant occupied an entire city block. Originally built during the 20s or 30s, the New Orleans facility integrated newer technology and changing customer requirements into production, necessarily forsaking efficiency. Much of the equipment was either deteriorating or obsolete. Moreover, producing the newly required double-lined containers entailed running the drums through the line twice. Floor space was limited, and there were no empty lots near the facility on which to expand. While restructuring and upgrading the facility would have required a four-month shutdown, there were other problems indigenous to the location.

Because of the facility's urban location, raw steel was unloaded from boxcars in the same small shipping and receiving area where finished goods were loaded onto trailers. Traffic congestion to and from the facility was heavy through New Orleans' narrow streets. While the proposed Canton building square footage was only slightly greater than at New Orleans (98,400 versus 96,265 square feet), the building was located on 9.5 undeveloped acres.

The raw steel was stored in the lower portion of the facility. Heavy rains and inadequate city storm sewage systems led to periodic flooding, causing the raw steel to rust. New Orleans' high humidity also caused rust. In an effort to combat the local weather problems, the New Orleans facility used oiled, rather than dry, steel. Before oiled steel can be used in fabrication, the oil must be chemically removed via a process that occasionally damages the steel's exterior coating. Oil residual results in either the lining or paint not adhering to the steel.

The sum of these difficulties at Inland's New Orleans facility was decreased capacity utilization due to weather or equipment failures, and a 40 percent product-quality rejection rate. The union conceded these difficulties, with one union official claiming, "there were more drums coming back in the plant [to be reworked] than going out."

NEW ORLEANS' LABOR-MANAGEMENT RELATIONS

Local 2179 represented Inland Container-New Orleans' workers since the 1940s, with the applicable contract effective October 1, 1980 to October 1, 1983 (see Exhibit 3, p. 144). Historically, Inland bargained jointly with the New Orleans, Cleveland, and Chicago container facilities, all of whom were categorized as List III steel fabricating plants. A provision within the national bargaining agreement mandated that Inland Container employees in List III plants receive the same basic wage and benefit package as unionized workers in Inland Steel's List I plants, their integrated steel manufacturing plants. As a result of this policy, plant-by-plant negotiations were normally confined to noneconomic issues.

Inland Container repeatedly attempted to remove all container facilities from List III in an effort to obtain competitive wages and benefits with non-List III companies or nonunion companies in their respective geographical or regional areas. In a letter dated October 15, 1981, the company addressed this concern:

> Our plants at Chicago, Cleveland and New Orleans are at a serious disadvantage in their efforts to compete in the steel pail and drum business due to their high labor rates. . . . They exceed by substantial amounts rates paid by our competitors—in many instances $3.00 to $4.00 per hour!
>
> The historical path of List III bargaining in our industry is littered with plant shutdowns and out-of-work steelworkers . . . I cannot stress the point too strongly—*these plants cannot survive if they are not allowed to become more cost competitive in the future.*

In January 1982, company officials met with union officials from the three List III container facilities, proposing wage and benefit reductions. The Cleveland local accepted Inland's proposal, voting for wage concessions in April 1982; both Chicago and New Orleans rejected the concessions. In an April letter, the latter facilities' union leadership formally advised Inland Container's president that they were "not prepared to meet relative to concessions on the existing contract."

In June, negotiations for a new national agreement commenced in Pittsburgh between the Coordinating Committee Steel Companies, of which Inland was a member, and the United Steelworkers of America. Inland again proposed that List III plants should not be governed by List I facility wage and benefit standards. The union executive board accepted Inland's proposal in November 1982, subject to membership ratification.

On November 2, 1982, Inland's industrial relations manager informally advised the union that closure was imminent. While the company representatives asserted that they enumerated all reasons for the decision, as well as the likelihood that operations would be moved elsewhere in the South, the union contended that management stressed high labor costs and did not reference their intention to transfer the work to another site. Moreover, the union objected to such a decision prior to the outcome of concession bargaining between the national negotiation teams.

In the letter dated November 3, Inland Container formally notified the union that:

> Pursuant to Section 10.13 of our collective bargaining agreement dated October 1, 1980, this is to notify you of the Company's intention to close permanently its New Orleans plant operations. . . . Representatives of the Company are prepared to meet with your representatives to discuss the proposed closure.
>
> Inland Steel Container strongly regrets that it must consider the permanent closing of its New Orleans plant. The cost of operations along with low volume and limitations of plant and facilities at the New Orleans plant make it impossible to justify continued operations.

Inland also posted a notice for employees regarding the intended closure, opening with: "I regret to inform you that we are going to permanently close the New Orleans plant. This shutdown is due to our inability to effectively compete because of high costs, plant and facility limitations, low volume and operating losses."

On November 29, the union contacted the company to discuss the intended closure. A meeting was scheduled for December 7 in the union's New Orleans office. While both parties agreed that during the meeting management discussed all facility limitations and problems, union representatives claimed management stressed that the closure was motivated by the high labor costs of the plant. Management contended, however, that problems in the plant were so pervasive that even labor cost relief would not solve the problems, despite the union's suggested concession bargaining. Nonetheless, company representatives indicated a willingness to review a union proposal.

Following the meeting, Inland Container's industrial relations manager wrote union representatives, stating, "It is essential that you let me know whether or not you intend to make a proposal by Monday, December 13, 1982, and if you are making a proposal that I have it by Friday, December 17, 1982." The union representative was on vacation, but learned of the letter via a telephone conversation with his secretary. He returned on December 16 but did not attempt to contact the company.

Having heard nothing from the union, Inland Container notified the union in a letter dated December 17 that it had made its final decision to close the New Orleans facility and proposed meeting with the union regarding effects of the shutdown. Three days later, Inland exercised the Canton purchase option.

In a letter dated January 3, 1983, the union responded to Inland's December 7 letter requesting union proposals. The union indicated that they were prepared "to discuss the terms and conditions to assure continued operations of the New Orleans plant or its shutdown should this be your final decision." The letter also noted, however, that: "Our union can point out to the company areas that could save the company many dollars in premium payments, but the company alone knows what is needed to assure continued operations of its plant in New Orleans. Therefore, it is only reasonable to understand that any proposals to assure the continued operations of the plant must come from the company."

Shortly after receiving the union's response, management contacted the union to arrange a meeting for discussing the effects of the shutdown and reaching a shutdown agreement. Prior to the scheduled meeting, a union staff representative contacted the industrial relations manager, asking whether wage concessions of three to four dollars per hour would save the plant. The manager responded negatively and discouraged any further union proposals for saving the plant.

During the scheduled January 28 meeting, the company advised the union that work would transfer to Canton. The union objected to moving New Orleans equipment. The union also raised their concern regarding the pending national concessions, feeling that soon-to-be-unemployed workers should not be dually penalized by accepting wage concessions in the final months. The final topics discussed at the meeting included transfers, pension, and vacation rights. Regarding transfers, the company asserted that New Orleans employees could transfer to Chicago but not Cleveland, which had recently broken with joint bargaining to sign a midcontract concession agreement, or Canton, which was not a List III facility.

At the next scheduled meeting, held February 17, Inland provided the union with their shutdown proposal. While the proposal excluded employees from any concessions being negotiated at the national level, the union objected to several other provisions of the proposal. The union objected to (1) termination of employee rights at the time of plant closing; (2) use of temporary employees following plant closure; and (3) an overtime provision allocating overtime compensation in accordance with federal laws (the 40-hour week guideline), versus the union proposal of time-and-a-half after eight hours of work.

A day or two following this meeting, a union representative telephoned a manager, stating that resolution of the overtime and rate-of-pay issues would finalize the shutdown agreement. As a result, Inland couriered to the union office a modified shutdown agreement addressing these two issues.

Around the same time, however, a United Steelworkers subdistrict director contacted local union officials, advising them that any shutdown agreement must include nonwaiver language, given the recent discovery that bargaining unit work was being transferred and that union members did not have transfer rights to the new facility. The union proposed that the following be added: "Nothing in this memorandum should be construed as a waiver of either parties' legal rights." The union claimed such nonwaiver language protected it from potential lawsuits from its members. By way of example, a union spokesperson contended that an employee three months short of pension eligibility might hold the union responsible for loss of benefits under the proposed shutdown agreement. The company countered that their proposed agreement contained specific provisions for such disputes, and that nonwaiver language would merely increase the likelihood of post-move lawsuits. The parties met or corresponded on the disputed language over the next several months, without resolution.

On August 12, 1983, Inland Container posted a notice at the New Orleans facility, inviting employees to apply for positions within the new Canton facility, expected to be operational about October 1 of that year.

QUESTION

At the time of the case, was Inland Container obligated to bargain with the union regarding the proposed shutdown?

EXHIBIT 1 Inland Steel Corporation—Results of Principal Operations, 1981 and 1982 (dollars in millions)

Business Segment	Sales			Profit (Loss)	
	1982	1981		1982	1981
Integrated steel	$1,874	$2,590		$(191)	$56
Steel service center	710	881		8	39
Construction products	184	238		7	11
Shipping containers	108	123		2	4
Shelter operations	98	109		(3)	1

Source: 1982 Annual Report.

EXHIBIT 2 Inland Steel Corporation—Principal Operations Investment, 1978–1982 (dollars in millions)

	1982	1981	1980	1979	1978
Integrated steel					
Assets	$2,130	$2,295	$2,359	$2,176	$1,999
Depreciation	114	150	133	118	104
Capital expenditures	75	116	221	262	252
Steel service center					
Assets	266	298	266	278	235
Depreciation	5	6	5	5	5
Capital expenditures	14	11	13	15	6
Construction products					
Assets	62	81	94	97	91
Depreciation	2	3	3	2	2
Capital expenditures	2	2	3	3	2
Shipping containers					
Assets	30	33	32	33	31
Depreciation	2	2	2	2	2
Capital expenditures	2	2	2	2	2
Shelter operations					
Assets	94	103	102	118	121
Depreciation	2	1	2	2	2
Capital expenditures	2	3	2	2	1

Source: 1982 Annual Report.

EXHIBIT 3   Applicable Contract Provisions

Section 1.2 Scope of Agreement: This agreement relates only to the plants of the Company located in Alsip, Illinois; Cleveland, Ohio; and New Orleans, Louisiana.

Section 2.2 Management Rights: Subject to the provisions of this Agreement, the management of the plants and direction of the working forces, including the right to hire, suspend, or discharge for proper cause, or promote, demote, or transfer, to schedule working hours and shifts, the right to relieve employees from duty because of lack of work or other reasonable causes, and to introduce new or improved production methods or facilities, are vested in the Company.

Section 10.13 Notice of Closure: Before the Company shall finally decide to close permanently a plant or discontinue permanently a department of a plant it shall give the Union, when practicable, advance written notification of its intention. Such notification shall be given at least 90 days prior to the proposed closure date, and the Company will thereafter meet with the appropriate representative in order to provide them with an opportunity to discuss the Company's proposed course of action. Upon conclusion of such meetings, which in no event shall be less than 30 days prior to the proposed closure or partial closure date, the Company shall advise the Union of its final decision. The final closure decision shall be the exclusive function of the Company. This notification provision shall not be interpreted to offset the Company's rights to lay off or in any other way reduce or increase the working force in accordance with its presently existing rights as set forth in Section 2.2 of this Agreement.

Weirton Steel and the Independent Steelworkers Union

By late 1982, Weirton Steel's joint labor-management study committee, McKinsey & Company, and Lazard Freres Company consultants had spent nine months negotiating the details of an employee stock ownership plan (ESOP) with both Weirton workers, represented by the Independent Steelworkers Union, and National Steel Corporation. If negotiations failed or employees failed to ratify the agreement, Weirton's future as a business would be jeopardized.

The Weirton team and National disagreed on two key items: the true value of Weirton's $370 million book-valued assets, and which company would assume the unfunded $100 million National pension liability attributable to Weirton employees, 2,500 of whom were already eligible to receive pension benefits.

If Weirton and National could resolve these issues, worker approval was still uncertain. The McKinsey consultants recommended a 32 percent cut in total employment compensation. Moreover, of the initial 12-member board of directors, only three seats would be filled by union representatives, with no employee voting rights until 1989.

NATIONAL STEEL CORPORATION

In early 1982, National Steel Corporation was the fourth largest domestic steel producer (see Exhibit 1, p. 150). Responding to industry trends, National was diversified with financial services and aluminum operating

*The authors wish to thank Mr. Ralph Cox, Weirton Steel Corporation, for his assistance and feedback on this case.

units, although steelmaking remained its core business (see Exhibits 2 and 3, pp. 151–152). To upgrade steel facilities, National infused over $1 billion in capital between 1976 and 1981. As steel demand continued to decline, however, National reduced or closed various operations. As of May 1980, 3,000 employees were on temporary or indefinite layoff, predominantly from National's Great Lakes steel division near Detroit, and 3 of National's 10 blast furnaces had been closed; the others were running at reduced capacity. In September 1981, National closed another blast furnace at Weirton Steel Division. By January 1981, National's Steel Group employment was down 6,000 persons from year-earlier levels, although growth in other National operating groups offset this reduction (see Exhibit 2, p. 151).

In 1982, National closed Hanna Furnace, their New York pig iron plant, and a related coke facility; sold or wrote off excess iron ore and coal properties; planned to sell the majority of assets of their National Steel Products Company subdivision, thus exiting the preengineered steel buildings, grain bins, windows, and doors customer segments; and offered Weirton Steel Division employees the opportunity to buy out National's interest in Weirton. Total 1982 National employment was 6,100 persons below year-end 1981 levels.

The proposed sale of Weirton would reduce National assets by $300 million (see Exhibit 4, p. 153), leaving National with an annual steelmaking capacity of 5.5 million tons from three modern steel mills with lower costs and good market positions.

WEIRTON STEEL DIVISION

Weirton Steel Division comprised one third of National Steel Corporation's 1981 annual steelmaking capacity and contributed $1.3 billion and $10 million to National's sales and net income, respectively. This earnings contribution, however, did not offset the $150 million National invested in Weirton between 1979 and 1981. Moreover, National realized in early 1982 that Weirton required an immediate $85 million to $110 million investment to comply with Environmental Protection Agency rules and to clean up factory water effluents. Additional capital would be required for maintenance, repair, and equipment upgrade. Also, Weirton's primary products were high-quality tinplate for the container industry and steel sheet for a variety of customers, all of which faced declining demand. New-product development demanded still more capital.

Another key contributor to Weirton's poor financial performance was that it had the highest employment costs in the industry: Weirton workers earned, on average, $27.60 per hour in wages and benefits, compared with the steel industry average of $24.70. The premium dated back to

Weirton's early history. In 1933, the United Steelworkers lost an attempt to organize Weirton, whose workers were represented by the Independent Steelworkers Union. In a company effort to thwart any future USW campaigns, Weirton workers garnered a wage premium well above the industry wage package. In return, the Weirton labor-management relations climate remained peaceful and strike-free while the rest of the steel industry faced bitter, extended USW strikes and resultant inventory stockpiling and customer loss.

National doubted it could gain significant concessions from the Independent Steelworkers in order to make production more competitive or Weirton more attractive to outside buyers. Second, the cost of capital for the required improvements would also discourage outside purchasers. Third, Weirton's older workforce comprised a substantial portion of National's total unfunded pension liability.

In January 1982, the Weirton pension fund liabilities exceeded pension fund assets of $350 million by $102 million. This $102 million difference accounted for almost half of National's entire corporate unfunded pension liability (see Exhibit 5, p. 154), as Weirton's employment accounted for a third of all National employees, and the average Weirton worker had been on the job 20 years. An immediate shutdown, however, would cost National an estimated $770 million in pensions and severance pay.

In March 1982, National proposed that Weirton employees buy the plant themselves. Shortly after National proposed the sale to employees, six local Weirton management personnel and 20 Independent Steelworkers union representatives formed a joint study committee charged with assessing the feasibility of employee ownership. Because Weirton was West Virginia's largest single employer and a large source of tax revenue, the state contributed $125,000 toward a McKinsey & Company ESOP feasibility study.

EMPLOYEE STOCK OWNERSHIP PLANS (ESOPS)

The idea of ESOPs originated in the 1950s with the introduction of Kelso plans. Subsequent tax laws[1] included favorable ESOP provisions, thus encouraging more and more companies to adopt ESOPs in an effort to improve company performance.

ESOPs are essentially defined contribution benefit plans. One differentiation of ESOPs from other benefit plans is that ESOPs invest primarily in company stock. As only the contribution formula is specified (either 15 percent or 25 percent of total annual salary depending upon

---

[1]Employee Retirement Income Security Act of 1974, the Tax Reduction Act of 1975, and the Economic Recovery Act of 1981.

financing), not the benefit (for example, 6 percent return on investment), the risk of return is borne by employees. Thus, employees as owners are supposedly motivated to make the business profitable. Moreover, as the employees have a long-term interest in the company, management is not driven by short-term stock price fluctuations. Another advantage of eliminating outside investors and their demands for dividends and earnings is that the ESOP's income must only equal operating costs.

ESOPs, again uniquely, are either nonleveraged or leveraged. Nonleveraged ESOPs, comprising approximately two thirds of all existing ESOPs, are defined as stock-bonus plans that purchase company stock with internal funds. However, ESOPs are also the only type of ERISA-qualified defined contribution plan that can leverage (use credit to finance) the purchase of company stock.

The financing must be a term loan, not a demand loan, and the interest rate must be deemed reasonable by the IRS. The company secures the loan with ESOP contributions equal to the loan payments. As the loan is repaid, stock is released to individual employee suspense accounts.[2] All ESOP loan proceeds must be used to either buy new shares of company stock (to raise capital) or purchase existing shares (to buy out owners). Were a company to default, the lender's only recourse is limited to the collateral pledged (that is, the ESOP trust, which doesn't include individual employee accounts); contributions made to the ESOP for repayment and those contributions' earnings; and cash dividends on the employer's stock.

For both nonleveraged and leveraged ESOPs, employers receive tax deductions for contributions to the ESOP, as well as dividends paid on ESOP stock. The ESOP trust for employee contributions is exempt from tax on income generated by the assets, and plan participants are not taxed on ESOP income until distributions are received (in other words, at retirement).

Leveraged ESOPs, however, have further tax advantages. For instance, nonleveraged ESOPs may deduct only up to 15 percent annual payroll to the ESOP trust, whereas leveraged ESOPs may deduct up to 25 percent of annual payroll. When leveraged, this 25 percent tax deduction essentially repays loan principal with pretax dollars. Moreover, interest paid on the loan is also tax deductible. Because of these tax advantages, leveraged ESOPs are used for a variety of business applications: raising new capital, refinancing existing debt, acquiring other companies, divesting company divisions, or taking a public company private.

While ESOPs' federal requirements and tax advantages are specific, the success of ESOPs as employee motivators varies. While some ESOP

---

[2]Any distribution of benefits, however, commences only after the loan is fully repaid.

firms increase annual employment growth and sales revenues above industry averages, others eventually file for Chapter 11 despite early gains. ESOP success appears to vary with the extent of employee involvement activities (preferably in conjunction with a participatory management structure), the motivations for establishing an ESOP, and whether the original company was publicly or privately held. The historical labor-management relations climate is also important; long-term adversaries may find it difficult to work cooperatively as co-owners.

RESULTS OF THE MCKINSEY STUDY

McKinsey reported back to the joint study committee in July 1982. In order to be competitive in the industry, Weirton's overall goal was to become one of the lower-cost producers of flat-rolled steel. In order to achieve this goal, McKinsey recommended two key employment changes: (1) eliminate over 400 management slots; and (2) while maintaining current hourly workforce levels, all workers (management and hourly) must accept a two-prong wage and benefit reduction of 32 percent. McKinsey recommended a 20 percent compensation reduction in order to keep Weirton operational. They further recommended an additional 12 percent cut for no more than four years. The total 32 percent compensation reduction would hopefully interest lenders, generating roughly $128 million annually in cost reductions, offsetting the anticipated $1.7 billion cash flow requirements over the next decade. However, if the rest of the steel industry gained wage and benefit concessions during subsequent negotiations, Weirton workers would need to reduce their compensation even further to remain competitive.

Part of the anticipated cash flow requirements included compliance with the federal environmental regulations. Other recommendations included installation of a second continuous caster, relining one of the four blast furnaces and a major rebuild on another, and the purchase of new coking ovens.[3]

The joint study committee then moved to explain the proposed cuts to the workers, holding a series of meetings in local public facilities and at various departments around the plant. The committee also hired the legal firm of Willkie Farr & Gallagher to assist in negotiating the buyout from National, and the investment banking firm of Lazard Freres to assist in arranging financing.

---

[3]National had closed Weirton's 87-oven coke battery in August 1982, relying on outside coke suppliers rather than expending for needed repairs and upgrading.

QUESTION

Under what conditions should workers accept the ESOP? What factors would you envision becoming important if the ESOP is accepted?

EXHIBIT 1   National Steel Corporation Summary of Operations, 1977–1981 (dollars in billions)

	1981	1980	1979	1978	1977
Net sales	$4.06	$3.71	$4.23	$3.75	$3.16
Total income	4.18	3.94	4.31	3.79	3.19
Cost of sales	3.88	3.67	3.90	3.38	2.92
Net income	.88	.85	1.26	1.12	.60
Net income (percent of sales)	2.1%	2.3%	3.0%	3.0%	1.9%
Total assets	$3.44	$3.45	$3.16	$2.85	$2.76
Total employment costs	1.31	1.23	1.26	1.13	.98
Employees	32,976	33,856	38,755	37,170	36,562
Raw steel production*	8.2	7.6	10.7	10.5	10.4
Shipments*	6.6	6.6	8.3	8.2	7.6

* Millions of net tons.

Source: 1982 Annual Report.

EXHIBIT 2 National Steel Corporation 1981 Business Segment Data (dollars in millions)

	Steel	Fabricating and Manufacturing	Aluminum	Corporate and General	Intersegment Eliminations	Total
Revenues						
Net sales	$3,489	$603	$226		$257	$4,062
Equity in earnings of associated companies	24	0.6	(8)	1		18
Other, including property sales	55	3	8	17		85
Total Revenues	3,568	607	226	19	257	4,165
Operating Profit	83	24	19	3		130
Identifiable assets	2,660	186	192	406		3,444
Depreciation	140	8	6	4		158
Capital expenditures	168	13	5	0.3		186

Source: 1981 Annual Report.

EXHIBIT 3   National Steel Corporation, 1981 Steel Group Results

Financial Results
(in millions)

Net sales	$3,489.0
Percent of corporate	86
Operating profit	$83.4
Percent of corporate	56

Steel Division
Shipments
(millions of tons)

Service centers	1.39
Containers	1.32
Automotive	1.19
Construction	.66
Pipe and tube	.73
Other	1.32
Total	6.6

Steel Production
by Process

Basic oxygen furnace	93%
Electric furnace	7
Total	100%
Continuous casting	48%

Source: 1981 Annual Report.

EXHIBIT 4 National Steel Corporation 1981 Balance Sheet
(dollars in thousands)

Assets

Current Assets:

Cash	$ 25,271
Short-term investments	11,864
Receivables	530,807
Recoverable income taxes	12,875
Deferred income taxes	47,126
Inventories/work-in-process	313,233
Inventories/raw materials	264,117
Total Current Assets	$ 1,205,293

Investments and Other Assets:

United Financial Corporation	281,127
Associated companies	
Capital stocks	130,291
Notes, debentures, advances	15,431
Miscellaneous investments	34,162

Properties:

Production and related facilities	3,171,628
Raw material, plant, and equipment	611,900
Transportation facilities	62,480
Less depreciation, depletion	(2,085,525)
Deferred Charges	17,106
Total Assets	$ 3,443,893

Liabilities and Stockholders' Equity

Current liabilities:

Bank notes	$ 40,000
Accounts payable	317,243
Salaries and wages	132,163
Withheld and accrued taxes	89,675
Pension and employee benefits	136,500
Other accrued items	35,675
Income taxes	33,164
Long-term obligations due within one year	47,244
Total Current Liabilities	$ 831,644
Long-term obligations	676,735

Deferred Credits:

Deferred income taxes	337,554
Insurance and miscellaneous reserves	88,233
Minority Interest in Subsidiaries	17,510

Stockholders' Equity:

Common stock at par value (19,780,674 shares)	98,903
Additional paid-in capital	134,689
Retained earnings	1,287,626
Less common stock held in treasury	(29,021)
Total liabilities and stockholders' equity	$ 3,443,893

Source: 1981 Annual Report.

EXHIBIT 5   National Steel Corporation 1980 and 1981 Pension Accounting

Thousands of Dollars	*1981*	*1980*
Actuarial present value of accumulated plan benefits:		
Vested	$1,001,870	$888,021
Nonvested	13,345	12,088
Total	$1,015,215	$900,109
Assets available for benefits	$ 792,947	$743,938
Unfunded liability	$ 208,923	$144,083

Source: 1981 Annual Report.

Xerox and the Amalgamated Clothing and Textile Workers' Union

Haloid Corporation, a manufacturer of specialty photographic paper, was founded in 1906 by four Rochester businessmen, some of whom were formerly employed by Eastman-Kodak. Under the guidance of Gilbert Mosher, elected president in 1917, Haloid built a strong sales force. The 1930 development of a superior photocopy paper and the 1935 purchase of Rectigraph Company, a manufacturer of photocopy machines, enabled Haloid to be the first company offering a complete line of photocopy products and service.

By the end of World War II, Haloid found itself within a cost-competitive market. Then president, Joseph C. Wilson, grandson of one of the founders, determined that Haloid must break new ground but also realized that Haloid had little internal funds by which to research and develop new products. To resolve this dilemma, Wilson lobbied the Battelle Memorial Institute to allow Haloid to license xerography, an electrostatic-photographic copying process patented by Chester Carlson in 1940 and supported by Battelle since 1944. Although small, Haloid claimed the technical expertise within the Rectigraph Division to develop a use for the patented process. Besides, IBM, RCA, and Kodak had already turned down Battelle's invitations to develop xerography. In 1947, Battelle conceded, and Haloid agreed to pay an 8 percent royalty on all sales of xerographic products and 62 percent of any royalties earned by licensing xerography to other firms. In 1948 this licensing agreement was amended to give Haloid permanent and exclusive rights to all xerographic products.

With a unique process, Haloid focused on application of xerography within the photocopy market. Between 1953 and 1960, Haloid expended over $70 million toward the development of xerographic products. In 1956, Haloid formed a joint venture with London-based Rank Organisation Ltd. to manufacture and market xerographic products worldwide. In 1960, the company introduced the 914, the first fully automatic dry copier. Unfortunately, the 914 calculated sale price would be 100 times that of competing copiers. As a result, the copier was available for lease only, a pricing practice that continued until the mid-70s.

In 1961, the company became Xerox Corporation, and Rank-Xerox formed a joint venture with Fuji Photo Film Company to penetrate the Far East market. Between 1960 and 1962, company sales nearly tripled, establishing Xerox as the market leader in the copier field.

As company revenues and profits exploded following the introduction of the 914, the Xerox organizational structure struggled to keep up. Between 1960 and 1971, the number of domestic employees grew from 9,000 to 63,000. While accommodating this growth, there was little time to develop managers in-house; Xerox sought managers for high-level positions from outside the company, mostly from Ford, GM, and IBM. By 1971 the average Xerox employee was less than 30 years old, and more than a third of all employees had been with the company fewer than three years.

The organizational structure shifted continually during the 60s, with copier sales and diversification, not efficiency, driving the shifts. In the early 60s, Xerox moved toward a divisional structure, reorganizing the sales division by product line, while maintaining central organization within research and development. Xerox underwent a major reorganization in 1966, again a mixture of product-line organization and staff-related functional organization. In 1969, the international division was formed following the purchase of the 51st percent of Rank-Xerox, and corporate headquarters moved from near the Rochester Business Products production facilities to Stamford, Connecticut. As a result, Xerox returned to the essentially central organization for domestic business in the early 70s, with many Rochester functional groups reporting to executives in Stamford.

THE SEVENTIES

The 70s hallmarked the end of Xerox's technical and marketing dominance of copiers and the beginning of a highly competitive copier industry. Following a decade of unprecedented growth, the 70s started with Xerox maintaining a 96 percent market share, and IBM's introduction of its first plain paper copier, Copier I. While not as sophisticated a machine as Xerox's 7000, Copier I was the offering of the preeminent IBM and posed a significant market threat in the office products field. Xerox responded by filing a law suit the same day, claiming IBM's infringement on 22 patents and violation of trade secrets disclosed during an earlier attempted joint venture. Xerox's defensive posture for the balance of the decade was set. IBM filed a countersuit. SCM launched a monopoly complaint, which the FTC formally adopted in 1973. Numerous other suits ensued, Xerox's legal staff burgeoned, executive time was devoted to depositions and court testimony, and Xerox became conservative in pricing policies to avoid potential legal retribution.

In addition to the legal battles over market dominance, Xerox faced unprecedented product competition as the 70s unfolded. Although Xerox expended heavily on R&D (see Exhibit 1, p. 166), their new product strategy and product development structure inhibited new products from being brought to market. The R&D functions (product planning, engineering, and manufacturing) were separate departments, with final authority at the corporate level. There were functional groups within each of these departments, each with its own hierarchy and functional responsibility. While this structure was intended to prevent mistakes from being marketed, it mainly inhibited any products from getting to the marketplace; those that were pushed out the door were normally at higher cost and behind schedule.

This new-product development inefficiency left Xerox vulnerable to new entrants. In addition, the selenium drum and other key Xerox patents expired in 1973, allowing numerous competitors to flood the market. By 1980, 147 plain paper copiers had been introduced in the United States. Two of note were Kodak, with a technically sophisticated copier, and Savin, with a reliable, inexpensive copier.

When Kodak introduced the Ektaprint in 1975, Xerox's retaliatory developments could not get through their R&D development maze. For example, the same year as the Ektaprint introduction, Xerox invested heavily in project Moses, which featured greater speed and a document feed that recycled originals. Before Xerox could get the bugs out of the new document feed, Kodak introduced a similar feed in 1976, and Moses was scrapped. Xerox's preeminence as the xerographic technology leader eroded.

Xerox's new-product development also failed to respond when Savin introduced a reliable $5,000 copier for sale only, targeted at the low-volume market. None of Xerox's new products was targeted toward this segment, estimated to be only 30,000 machines total; all but one new-product introduction since the 914 stressed increased speed or features, aimed at the mid- to high-volume user (see Exhibit 2, p. 167). The potential of the low-volume market had been greatly underestimated, and Savin's annual sales surpassed 50,000 copiers.[1]

---

[1] By the end of the decade, 14 other Japanese competitors entered the copier market with low-volume machines, including Canon, Sharp, and Minolta, gradually expanding product offerings into the mid-volume range. Combined, Japanese competitors placed 200,000, 400,000, and 500,000 copiers in the United States in 1976, 1977, and 1978 respectively.

With no low-volume copier to offer in competition, Xerox's immediate response to Savin's entry involved a fundamental shift in their marketing policy: Xerox started offering their machines for sale instead of lease only (see Exhibit 3, p. 167). While selling machines increased current revenues despite Xerox's diminishing market share, there was concern within the company that long-term cash flow would be jeopardized. In addition, having decided to sell copiers, Xerox initiated a price war in 1976 in an effort to stave off Japanese competition. This price competition lasted through the rest of the decade, resulting in new management focus on reducing production costs.

While continually battling competition in an effort to regain reprographic market share, Xerox also continued diversification attempts into less competitive product lines. Diversification attempts started with the purchase of University Microfilms in the early 60s and expanded to include entry into magnetics (1960s), electro-optical defense/aerospace (1960s), mainframe computers (1969), specialized computer hardware (1977), various publishing-related subsidiaries (1978 and 1979), data transfer (1979), and miscellaneous computer products (1980). None of these attempts, however, affected reprographics' contribution to the Xerox income statement. In 1979, Xerox Credit Corporation was formed, the first financial diversification for the company.

In spite of all these efforts, by 1980 Xerox's market share was 45 percent, less than half of its 1970 share. Responding to the stiff Japanese competition, management attention turned to streamlining the organizational structure that slowed product development and reducing actual production costs of existing as well as planned products. Accomplishing these goals, however, would still leave Xerox vulnerable to shrinking margins within reprographics. Hence, Xerox renewed its commitment to identifying and diversifying into more profitable product lines. Xerox's involvement in financial services extended with the 1982 announcement of plans to acquire Crum & Forster insurance organizations.

PRODUCTION—JAPAN

Japanese firms proudly conducted tours through their copier production facilities. Spending the bulk of investment in engineering designs and software development, Japanese firms opened the doors of their highly automated facilities with little fear of losing their competitive edge. Facilities were immaculate and dimly lit, the only movement on the shop floor being robots transfering components and subassemblies from station to station. With each delivery, robots emitted signals, triggering parts flows in other areas of the plant. A handful of computer technicians supervised the entire operation, overseeing production from a control booth above the shop floor.

The Japanese reputation for commitment to its workers remained unscathed by the high degree of automation; firms such as Canon and Minolta entered into copier production during the 70s while maintaining original workers in their other product lines. Most firms entered the copier industry with fully automated production facilities.

PRODUCTION—XEROX

Most reprographic equipment is produced within the seven plants of the Webster, New York, complex (see Exhibit 4, p. 167). Each plant houses some combination of the nine Xerox production-related groups: New-Build, MSMMO (materials), Model Shop, Distribution, Maintenance, Central Refurbishing Centers, Fabrication, Sub-Assembly, and Off-Set.

Materials

In 1968, Xerox, already aware of the need to control the flow of production parts within New-Build, began devising a materials requirement planning (MRP) system to track the flow of components. By 1974, all four facilities within the Information Systems Group, charged with the the manufacture, distribution, and servicing of office duplicators and copiers in the United States, had production and inventories planned and controlled by their in-house MRP system.

The system, however, was programmed according to sales projections, with many supplier orders made well in advance of actual production need. During the 1974–75 recession, parts inventories accumulated; at one point inventories were 40 percent above what was needed. Xerox's first response was to move from an order-by-order purchasing system to consolidation of commodity parts orders and longer-term contracts with suppliers. These two decisions yielded a 21 percent savings for the company. They also led to an organizational change. Historically, a team of materials analysts was assigned to a given plant within a given product line. Several different products, however, often contained the same part (called a commodity part), and that same part would be ordered by several different teams. In 1976 teams were consolidated by commodity group so that a given part supplier worked with only one group. Consequently, Materials Management became more centralized.

In the early 80s, the Materials Management organization changed again, extending the sole-supplier concept into actual new-product development, as well as adding engineers to the commodity teams. Xerox also invested in extensive training of suppliers in their statistical process control techniques. In addition, they implemented the early supplier involvement program, calling for exchange-of-information with numerous suppliers in an effort to improve Xerox's ability to produce new products, and a given supplier's ability to supply parts according to Xerox's production demands.

Another significant change in materials management accompanied Xerox's adoption of a just-in-time (JIT) inventory control system, meant to accomplish two main goals: (1) the reduction in on-hand inventory and materials for production, and (2) the minimizing of inventory handling. Xerox spent $45 million to automate materials-handling, as well as some assembly operations, in conjunction with the requirement that vendors ship materials only as they are needed by the factory. From 1980 to 1982, these changes in the inventory system saved Xerox over $100 million.

Labor History

In March 1937, a sit-down strike by Haloid workers effectively communicated to management that employment conditions were not satisfactory. Moreover, the independent strikers requested and gained the support of the largest local union in the area: Local 14A of the Amalgamated Clothing Workers (later renamed the Amalgamated Clothing and Textile Workers). After the strike, the workers, comprising about 10 percent of Haloid's total employees, organized under Local 14A, and negotiated their first contract with Haloid.

Management resented the organization of the workers, and the early years of labor-management relations were stormy. Not until the mid-50s, when Joseph C. Wilson succeeded his father as CEO, did the Labor Relations Department within Haloid become a fully integrated part of the corporate structure. Under the younger Wilson's guidance, a new labor-management philosophy was laid down: management would recognize workers' interests as legitimate, and Haloid would strive for the betterment of both the company and the labor force. Moreover, management would respect workers' desire to have a standard of living equal to or better than other area or industry workers. Wilson also instituted an open-door policy for union leaders at the Webster facilities and effectively acted as an arbitrator of unresolvable disputes between Haloid's middle management and local union leaders. For almost two decades, labor-management relations were peaceful.

In the early 70s, implementation of the MRP system led to consolidation of plant managements, with increased pressure on labor to reduce costs. In 1973, the conflict resulted in Xerox's first strike since the 1937 sit-down that heralded in the union. While the strike was short and workers returned with a package similar to that offered before the strike, it was an important display that the union was still willing to exercise its perogatives in the event of disagreements during negotiations. More-over, the strike held up production of two new product introductions: the compact 3100 and the automatic Telecopier 410. According to one union spokesman, "They didn't think we'd walk out; we didn't think they'd let us. Because of the strike, management knew it couldn't take us for granted."

In 1974, inflation and shrinking markets slowed Xerox's growth. Al-though the company and Rank Organisation Ltd. announced plans to open two European plants for the production of copiers and duplicators, domestic production ebbed. By the end of the year Xerox had closed some Webster facilities, displacing 6,000 New York employees. Through 1975, heavy U.S. layoffs of both white- and blue-collar employees con-tinued. In 1976, Xerox stopped offering both new and remanufactured units of some older copier models in the United States. In mid-1977, Xerox revealed plans to invest $20 million in its Brazilian plant in order to manufacture the new 3107 compact copier. Domestic layoffs continued into the early 1980s.

The Employee Involvement Program

In March 1980, Local 14A, representing 4,000 hourly employees, and Xerox agreed during negotiations to introduce a quality of work-life (QWL) process in three manufacturing groups (New Build, Materials, and Maintenance) within four of Xerox's plants in Webster, New York. The added contract provision called for the establishment of a joint company-union employee involvement committee, charged with pur-suing opportunities to enhance employee work satisfaction and increase productivity.

The union was skeptical but agreed to the effort as long as participation was voluntary, the program was truly jointly controlled and monitored, and the program structure remained separate from either party's internal structure. Furthermore, program activities could not infringe upon the traditional collective bargaining relationship. Hence, contract language outlined those areas that the shop-floor problem-solving groups (PSGs) could and could not address.

Structure.   There are four organizational levels within the QWL pro-gram (see Exhibit 5, p. 168). The top Policy and Planning Committee was originally composed of four management and four union members. As Xerox's organizational structure has since decentralized, however, more management people sit on the committee. The committee estab-lishes broad guidelines as well as training and meeting requirements.

At the plant level is the Plant Advisory Committee (PAC), comprised of the plant manager, general foreman, technical staff, elected union officials, and hourly employees. The PAC is charged with implementing the Policy and Planning Committee's guidelines, assisting shop-floor groups in obtaining necessary information and expertise, implementing recommendations, and, finally, monitoring the overall progress of plant-level employee involvement activities.

Under the PAC are various departmental or "family" committees depending upon the needs of the unit. They are usually composed of the general foreman, department/family technical staff, an elected union official, and hourly employees from the department/family. These committees develop plans for establishing and implementing PSGs and coordinate and monitor various group activities across the department.

Within each department are numerous PSGs of employees that meet for about an hour each week. Generally, PSGs consist of six to eight hourly volunteer employees and their foreman or an elected group leader.

Coordination and Training. Eight management and eight union representatives were originally charged with providing the 40 hours of problem-solving and team-building training over a 10-week period for team members. These facilitators also provided groups with technical advice and assisted groups in getting recommendations implemented. Facilitators were under the jurisdiction of the plant advisory committees.

Group Activities. Acting much like quality circles, PSGs tend to focus on job-related problems and ways of improving company performance. Per the contract, PSGs are not allowed to focus on contractual language items, nor certain traditional management prerogatives (see Exhibit 6, p. 169). On average, PSGs find solutions within three and four months. To implement recommendations, PSGs present proposals to the Department/Family Steering Committee, and with their assistance send it up through the PAC, to the appropriate plant management level.

1980–1982 Expansion. Within two years, all seven plants in the Webster complex had engaged in the collaborative program, forming over 150 active problem-solving groups. Although on average problem resolution took only three or four months, some problems took over a year to resolve, and still others only served to frustrate group members due to the complexity of the issues. Also, because of extensive bumping and bidding rights within the contract, high group turnover undermined ongoing group efforts. During this same time, moreover, nearly 1,200 union members were laid off, exacerbating the turnover problem and increasing worker skepticism regarding management's commitment to employee welfare. Consequently, interest in the QWL program began to wane, and the number of new volunteers for QWL training declined in 1982.

In part the decline in participation was fueled by Xerox's 1981 announcement of plans to subcontract out the work of the Wire Harness

Department at a cost savings of $3.2 million, eliminating 180 jobs. Given the gravity of worker displacement and the impact that such a move would have on employee participation in future joint efforts, the union approached management requesting that an ad hoc team be established in an effort to provide management with an alternative to the subcontracting. Although subcontracting was clearly a management prerogative, and despite management's contention that they had already reviewed every in-house alternative, management agreed to establish a Study Action Team, giving it six months to come up with acceptable alternatives.

The team's task came at a time when Xerox had just completed an overhaul of its management strategies and objectives for the coming decade, including implementation of a benchmark program. Benchmarking set manufacturing and service cost ceilings in conjunction with design, reliability, and quality floors established by Xerox to meet or beat worldwide competition. Thus, the Study Action Team not only had to shave over $3 million in cost, but simultaneously meet the other benchmarking criteria.

The Study Action Team was comprised of six hourly workers from Wire Harness, an engineer, and a manager. The size of their task was enormous, skepticism reduced cooperation among other plant personnel, and organizational barriers made it difficult to interface with such management areas as finance and policy. A de facto split between the hourly and management team members became apparent. Top union leaders and upper management then intervened, hired an outside consultant, and the Study Action Team became functionally efficient.

At the end of the six-month allotted time, the team presented management with a plan that significantly exceeded the target $3.2 million in cost savings (see Exhibit 7, p. 169). While the largest single concentration of anticipated savings involved changes in the organizational structure, over 38 percent of the savings suggested were in areas covered by the contract: consolidating jobs and stabilizing labor by eliminating certain bidding rights. For example, at the time of the Study Action Team's recommendations, workers within Wire Harness transferred on average four times a year. The Study Action Team felt that a limit on the annual transfers would increase efficiency by reducing training costs, as well as reducing costs of the ripple effect associated with each transfer.

Those recommendations that did not involve contractual issues were implemented, the subcontracting decision was put on hold, and the balance of the recommendations would be addressed during the upcoming 1983 negotiations.

Organization and Management

In 1980, Xerox's indecisive management strategy and matrix organization involving production-related group heads reporting to separate corporate executives, crippled the company's ability to react offensively to increasing competition. As a result, Xerox underwent massive reorganization following implementation of the benchmarking strategy. The process was expected to take considerable time. As a result of initial resizing efforts, 12,500 employees were laid off between mid-1981 and year-end 1982, 1,200 of whom were union members. This total figure was partially offset by an increase in employment in electronic printing, electronic typewriter, and office systems businesses:

Xerox Worldwide Employment (all businesses)

1978	1979	1980	1981	1982
104,695	112,678	117,247	117,930	109,940

CURRENT NEGOTIATIONS ISSUES[2]

Early discussion between the parties has revealed that management sees reduced costs as key to remaining competitive, and union leadership views job and income security as a paramount membership concern. Each party, however, understands the dilemma and the genuine interests of the other. Bridging these conflicting interests within a mutually constructive agreement remains the key challenge of these negotiations.

Negotiations have been tough, tougher than any other that the negotiators can recall. The contract expired 10 days ago; facing a walkout, the parties agreed to extend negotiations for two weeks. Early last week, Local 14A tentatively conceded to new language controlling unexcused absences and co-payment provisions covering health-related benefits. In the last several days, however, there has been no movement on the remaining issues. Each side has dug in its heels.

Management hasn't budged from its initial demand for a wage freeze. It holds that a wage freeze is necessary to achieve competitiveness with the Japanese (who are selling compact copiers for less than Xerox's production cost), and to abate declining profitability within Reprographics (see Exhibits 8 and 9 , p. 170–171). Local 14A, on the other hand, demands some increase in wage rates, arguing that members had already accepted a wage freeze in the last round of negotiations. The union has been holding to its last demand of 5, 3, and 2 percent annual increases over the life of the three-year agreement.

Local 14A is painfully aware of the loss of over 150,000 jobs in the textile industry (the ACTWU's predominant industry) over the past de-

---

[2]This negotiation environment is fictitious, generated solely to frame case discussion, and is not intended to be reiterative of either management's or union's viewpoints at the 1983 negotiations.

cade despite wage levels only 60 percent of the manufacturing average. Closer to home, Rochester-based Eastman-Kodak recently announced employee layoffs, the first in that company's history. As a result, Local 14A has been demanding job security language protecting its members from any further layoffs. Management negotiators have offered job protection against displacement caused by the introduction of new technologies or by the implementation of any employee involvement recommendations. Management has been unwilling, on the other hand, to protect members from displacement as "dictated by reduced sales or competitive subcontracting." Indeed, management has promised in the near future to provide details of a subcontracting bid, potentially saving $4 to $5 million in yet another reprographic production department, Fabrication, despite current language limiting subcontracting. The decision would displace some 230 bargaining unit jobs.

Also yet to be resolved are several key disputes arising from the Study Action Team recommendations concerning the Wire Harness department. In particular, the Study Action Team made recommendations to

1. Redefine or consolidate job classifications so that natural work groups could operate as self-managing teams.
2. Restrict the frequency of voluntary employee transfers in or out of the department (based on companywide seniority rights) in order to stabilize work teams and reduce the direct costs and inefficiencies of such transfers.
3. More fully utilize temporary employees, at lower wage and benefit rates than full-time employees, during periods of upturns in production.

These three recommendations were expected to reduce operating costs by 11 percent, accounting for 39 percent of the total projected savings. Local 14A forestalled implementing the recommendations, however, as they infringed on 1980 contract language. Failing to implement the recommendations left the Study Action Team proposal significantly short of the original subcontracting bid.

As the parties wrestle with these key issues, much discussion focuses on both the successes and disappointments of the various jointly administered employee involvement activities. Most (but not all) members of both negotiating teams express continued, strong commitment to joint efforts. As a result, management and union leaders are distressed that employee enthusiasm for involvement activities is waning. In recent months, only one out of four nonparticipants has expressed any interest in becoming involved. Furthermore, many of the once-vocal supporters of QWL were beginning to question the utility of the program.

Management and union leaders agree that continued layoffs and permanent work-force reductions undermine worker enthusiasm for joint activities. Management negotiators further contend that QWL participants become frustrated when recommendations are not implemented, recommendations that would save their jobs despite contract infringement. While these members may not necessarily want the entire contract altered, they surely desire some departmental discretion when their very livelihood is at stake.

The union, on the other hand, argues that involvement waned appreciably when members realized that certain recommendations threatened the security offered within the contract. Although the recommended amendments to the contract within Wire Harness would not cost any member his or her job, a precedent of contractual leniency could result in job losses within other departments. Besides, since over 60 percent of the savings applied to areas of traditional management responsibility (such as overhead and equipment repair), the union contends that poor management, not the labor agreement, is at the root of Xerox's noncompetitiveness.

The parties decided to take a full day for internal caucusing. They are scheduled to reconvene negotiations tomorrow afternoon.

EXHIBIT 1   Xerox Research and Development Expenditures

Year	R&D Expense ($000)	R&D as Percent of Revenue
1960	3,119	8.4
1965	38,170	7.0
1970	87,000	5.1
1971	96,000	4.9
1972	117,000	4.9
1973	154,000	5.1
1974	179,000	5.0
1975	198,000	4.7
1976	226,000	5.0
1977	269,000	5.1
1978	311,000	5.1
1979	376,000	5.3
1980	418,000	5.4
1981	526,000	6.1
1982	541,000	7.0*

*Percentage figured on the basis of Business Products and Systems' revenues, not total company revenues.

Source: Annual Reports.

EXHIBIT 2   Copier Industry Segments (by volume)

Segment	Copies/Minute	Retail Price
Low volume	1–20	under $ 4,500
Mid volume	21–75	up to 20,000
Upper volume	75–90	up to 60,000
High volume	91 plus	up to 150,000

EXHIBIT 3   Rentals and Service versus Sales Revenues (000 omitted)

Year	Rental and Service	Sales
1970	$1,378	312
1971	1,599	355
1972	1,968	434
1973	2,500	485
1974	2,946	640
1975	3,401	739
1976	3,592	923
1977	3,826	1,369
1978	4,146	1,887
1979	4,637	2,390
1980	4,839	2,764
1981	4,761	3,045
1982	4,548	3,239

Source: Annual Reports.

EXHIBIT 4   Seven Facilities in Webster Complex

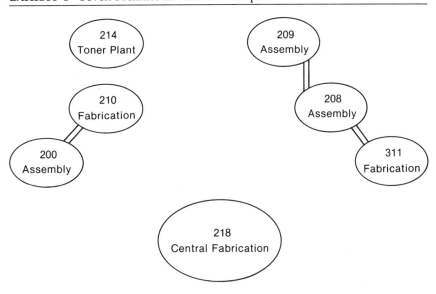

Source: Adapted from company records (configuration disguised to protect confidentiality).

EXHIBIT 5 Xerox: Webster Facilities, Quality of Work-Life Program Structure

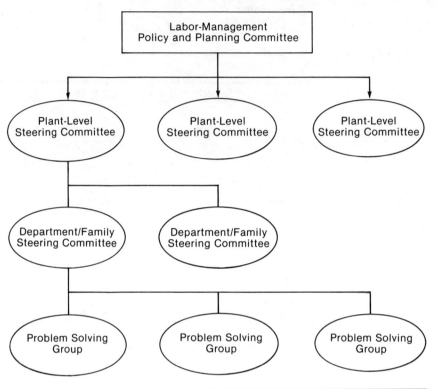

Source: Company Records.

EXHIBIT 6 Quality of Work-Life Program: Problem-Solving Group Boundaries

Off-Limits Areas	*Permissible Areas*
Salaries	Product quality
Union grievances	Work environment safety
Union contract	Savings in material and inventory costs
Benefits	Improvements in process, methods, or
Company policy	systems
Working hours	Improvements in facilities, tools, or
Rates	equipment
Breaks	Reduction in paperwork
Classification	Elimination of waste of materials and
Overtime	supplies
Personalities	Quality
Payroll	Scrap
Discipline	Rework
Problems shop chairmen are	Locations of equipment and materials
working on	
Production standards	

Source: Company Records.

EXHIBIT 7 Changes Recommended by Study-Action Team

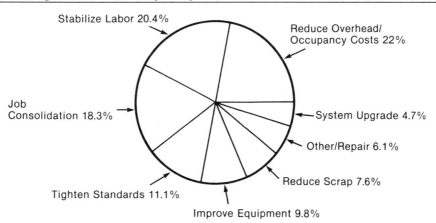

Total Savings = $3,642,000
(28.6% Total Departmental Budget)

Source: U.S. Department of Labor, Bureau of Labor-Management Relations and Cooperative Programs.

EXHIBIT 8 Financial Data by Industry Segment (in millions of dollars)

	Reprographics	Paper	Other Businesses	Eliminations	Consolidated
		1982			
Revenues	6,333	524	1,815	(216)	8,456
Transfers between segments	–	–	30	(30)	–
Total operating revenues	6,333	524	1,845	(246)	8,456
Operating Profit	1,22.	36	6		1,164
Expenses					(567)
Income taxes					(153)
Outside shareholders' interests					(76)
Income from continuing operations					368
Identifiable assets	4,954	213	1,572		
General assets					
Depreciation	707	9	97		
Capital expenditures	944	12	206		
		1981			
Revenues	6,393	555	1,706	(144)	8,510
Transfers between segments	–	–	37	(37)	–
Total operating revenues	6,393	555	1,743	(181)	8,510
Operating Profit	1,356	35	85		1,475
Expenses					(342)
Income taxes					(434)
Outside shareholders interests					(127)
Income from continuing operations					572
Identifiable assets	5,172	203	1,511		
General assets					
Depreciation	718	8	81		
Capital expenditures	1,202	11	188		
		1980			
Revenues					
Rentals and services	4,841	–	409	(98)	5,152
Sales	1,224	574	1,247	–	3,045
Transfers between segments	–	–	34	(34)	–
Total operating revenues	6,065	574	1,690	(132)	8,197
Operating Profit	1,326	44	125		1,495
Expenses					(216)
Income before income taxes					1,279
Identifiable assets	5,212	221	1,398		
General assets					
Depreciation	719	8	98		
Capital expenditures	1,108	13	192		

Source: 1981 and 1983 Annual Reports.

EXHIBIT 9   Financial Data by Geographic Area (in millions of dollars)

	United States	Rank Xerox Companies	Other Areas	Eliminations	Consolidated
		1982			
Revenue	$5,042	$2,454	$1,176	$(216)	$8,456
Transfers between geographic areas	374	17	44	(435)	–
Total operating revenues	5,416	2,470	1,220	(651)	8,456
Income before outside shareholders' interests	217	159	69	(7)	444
Outside shareholders' interests	–	(72)	(4)	–	(76)
Income from discontinued operations	56	–	–	–	56
Net income	273	87	64	(7)	424
Assets	4,193	2,196	1,336	(57)	7,668
		1981			
Revenue	$4,784	$2,681	$1,189	$(144)	$8,510
Transfers between geographic areas	259	13	61	(333)	–
Total operating revenues	5,043	2,694	1,251	(477)	8,510
Income before outside shareholders' interests	327	242	137	(6)	700
Outside shareholders' interests	–	(106)	(21)	–	(127)
Income from discontinued operations	26	–	–	–	26
Net income	352	136	116	(6)	598
Assets	4,379	2,342	1,023	(69)	7,674
		1980			
Revenue	$4,466	$2,856	$ 973	$(98)	$8,197
Transfers between geographic areas	223	4	45	(272)	–
Total operating revenues	4,688	2,860	1,018	(370)	8,197
Income before outside shareholders' interests	335	221	115	(4)	667
Outside shareholders' interests	–	(89)	(13)	–	(102)
Net income	335	132	102	(4)	565
Assets	4,017	2,724	831	(58)	7,514

Source: 1981 and 1983 Annual Reports.

Appendix   Selected 1980 Xerox-ACTWU Local 14A Contract Language

Article II.
Subcontracting

B1. The subcontracting policy of the Company shall be carried out subject to the following provisions:

    a. The Company reserves the right, except as otherwise limited by this Agreement, to make determinations as to where and how its production and other work requirements can best be provided. However, the Company recognizes an obligation toward its employees to use carefully considered judgment when it makes decisions to subcontract work.

    b. Upon request by the Union, the Company shall provide information to the Union regarding subcontracting activity. In addition, the Company shall provide to appropriate duly authorized shop representatives, on a monthly basis, a list of those job classifications in which employees had performed work currently being subcontracted.

  2. The Company shall designate a management committee which shall be comprised of the Vice President, Rochester Manufacturing Group, NAMD, the Corporate Industrial Relations Director, and other appropriate representatives of the Company. This committee shall meet with the Union at four (4) regularly scheduled quarterly meetings per year for purposes of reviewing subcontracting programs and plans. In addition, when requested by the Union, the management committee shall also meet with the Union for purposes of hearing specific cases involving subcontracting issues. Following review of the cases presented by the Union, the management committee shall direct that appropriate action be taken in meritorious cases to maintain a work volume which will allow stabilization of employment and wage levels where it is possible and practicable to do so in accordance with prevailing business conditions. Such action, however, shall not involve the company in forfeiture expenses, the need for capital investment, or the loss of its ability to meet production schedules. At the request of the Manager, Rochester Joint Board, A.C.T.W.U., special meetings shall be scheduled with the Company's President for purposes of discussing any matters relating to subcontracting which have not been resolved through discussions between the management committee and the Union.

Article V.
Wage Determination and Payment

A. JOB CLASSIFICATIONS.

    1. All job classifications of employees covered by this Agreement are assigned to labor grades as set forth in Schedule A., attached to this Agreement and made part of it.

    2. In the event of the creation of new job classifications covered by this Agreement, or changes in existing job classifications, the assignment of

such jobs into proper labor grades shall be in accordance with the provisions of Supplemental Agreement 3., attached to this Agreement and made part of it.

B. WAGES.

1. Hourly base rates during the term of this Agreement are set forth in Schedule B., attached to this Agreement and made part of it. Employees shall receive the hourly base rate of pay set forth for the labor grade of the job classification to which they are assigned. Employees assigned to job classifications in the Building Custodial Services Seniority Unit shall be paid a rate not less than that of Labor Grade 3.

E. COST-OF-LIVING ALLOWANCE.

1. Effective on March 24, 1980 and thereafter for the duration of the term of this Agreement, employees shall be covered by the cost-of-living allowance provisions set forth in this section.

2. The amount of the cost-of-living allowance shall be determined on the basis of the Consumer Price Index for Urban Wage Earners and Clerical Workers (revised), U.S. CITY AVERAGE, All Items, 1967 = 100, published monthly by the Bureau of Labor Statistics, U.S. Department of Labor, and referred to as the CPI-W.

3. The amount of the cost-of-living allowance shall be calculated for all employees on the basis of one (1) cent per hour for each .3 point change in the CPI-W, as measured by the point difference between the CPI-W for October 1976, and the CPI-W for the months indicated in Column 1., below: [omitted here].

Article VI.
Seniority

C. PROMOTIONS, TRANSFERS, CUTBACKS, AND DOWNGRADES.

1. Promotions, transfers, cutbacks, and downgrades shall be handled in each seniority unit in accordance with the provisions of the applicable Supplemental Agreement in the list below:

a. Manufacturing Seniority Unit—Supplemental Agreement A.

F. LAYOFF

1. Contrary to the provisions of any Promotion and Transfer Supplemental Agreement, Company seniority shall prevail across seniority units for the purpose of layoffs, except in those instances specifically cited below.

2. When it becomes necessary for the Company to lay off employees in the Manufacturing, Supplies Manufacturing, Service and Maintenance, and Building Custodial Services Seniority Units, it shall effectuate the layoffs through the following sequence:

a. The Company shall determine the total number of jobs to be eliminated in each of the seniority units affected and shall thereby determine the total number of employees to be laid off from the bargaining unit.

b. The Company shall then identify on a roster all employees in these seniority units in the order of their Company seniority.

c. The following employees shall be excluded from the roster:

(1) All employees in the following job categories:

(a) In the Manufacturing Seniority Unit, all job classifications:
    (i) With "W" lettered job codes.
    (ii) Of the Tool and Die Maker Apprentice Program.
    (iii) Of the Model Maker and Experimental Mechanic Apprentice Program.
(b) In the Service and Maintenance Seniority Unit all job classifications:
    (i) With "L" lettered job codes which are identified as Skilled Trades in Article X of this Agreement.
    (ii) Of all Maintenance Apprentice Programs.
(2) All employees in the Manufacturing, Service and Maintenance, and Supplies Manufacturing Seniority Units in job classifications of Labor Grade 12 or higher. . . .

d. Layoffs shall be effected in accordance with the following provisions:
(1) The roster, minus exclusions, shall be referred to as the adjusted roster and shall serve as the basis for effecting layoffs.
(3) The number of employees subject to involuntary layoffs shall be reduced by the number of employees subject to voluntary layoffs as described in F.,2.,d.,(4), of this Article.

Article XIV.
Employee Involvement

A Joint Company-Union Employee Involvement Committee shall be established to investigate and pursue opportunities for enhancing employees' work satisfaction and productivity. To this end, the Joint Committee shall meet regularly to undertake the following responsibilities:

A. Review and evaluate ongoing programs, projects, and experiments, both within and outside the Company, designed to encourage employee involvement.
B. Develop programs, projects, and experiments that might ultimately be broadly applied.
C. Establish subcommittees to develop suggested programs for specific areas. Hear and review reports from these subcommittees.
D. Submit reports and recommendations to the Company and Union regarding the implementation and subsequent progress of specific programs.

Schedule B.
Hourly Base Rates

Labor Grade		*Hourly Base Rates*		
	Effective:	03/24/80	03/23/81	03/22/82
1–2		$7.679	$7.909	$8.146
3		7.772	8.005	8.245
4		7.961	8.200	8.446
5		8.147	8.391	8.643
6		8.336	8.586	8.844
7		8.525	8.781	9.044
8		8.711	8.972	9.241

Schedule B.
Hourly Base Rates (*concluded*)

Labor Grade	Hourly Base Rates		
9	8.900	9.167	9.442
10	9.089	9.362	9.643
11	9.276	9.554	9.841
12	9.465	9.749	10.041
13	9.654	9.944	10.242
14	9.841	10.136	10.440
15	10.028	10.329	10.639
16	10.217	10.524	10.840
17	10.404	10.716	11.037
18	10.593	10.911	11.238
19	10.782	11.105	11.438
20	10.969	11.298	11.637
21	11.158	11.493	11.838
22	11.345	11.685	12.036
23	11.534	11.880	12.236
24	11.722	12.074	12.436
25	11.909	12.266	12.634
26	12.097	12.460	12.834

Supplemental Agreement A
Promotions, Transfers, Cutbacks, and Downgrades Within the Manufacturing
Seniority Unit

The Company and Union agree that this Supplemental Agreement and the Manufacturing Seniority Unit Promotion and Transfer Chart, as revised from time to time by agreement of the parties, shall serve as the basis for all job movements by employees in the Manufacturing Seniority Unit. Such job movements shall be made in accordance with the procedures described in this Supplementary Agreement.

1. DEFINITIONS

* * * *

N. Movement within Classification
   1. Voluntary: This Movement occurs when employees elect to change their Job Status.
      a. Level One Volunteer: This type of Volunteer is an employee who volunteers to move to an Opening with another Job Status, thereby eliminating the need for another employee, who does not wish to move, to do so.
      b. Level Two Volunteer: This type of Volunteer is an employee who volunteers to move to another Job Status held by another employee who is a Level One Volunteer.
      c. Preference Movement: This type of Voluntary Movement by an employee occurs within a Classification when a Promotion Condition exists in that Classification.

2. Involuntary: This type of Involuntary Movement occurs when employees are required to change their Job Status.

II. JOB PREFERENCE SHEET

A. In exercising their movement rights, employees shall indicate for Voluntary Upward Movement and Voluntary Movement Within Classification their choice of Job, Shift Mode, and Word Assignment. Employees shall indicate for Involuntary Movement Within Classification their Job, Shift Mode, and Geographic Location. Employees shall indicate for Involuntary Downward Movement their Job, Shift Mode and Production Center.

D. Movement Within, Into, and Out of Work Assignments. With regard to Movement Within Work Assignments, management shall be free to move employees, without resort to the procedures described in this Supplemental Agreement, so long as their permanent Shift Mode and Job are maintained. All other permanent movement shall take place only by following the procedures described in this Supplemental Agreement.

E. Movement methodology, as described in this Supplement, shall apply equally to all Classifications and all Work Assignments. This Movement methodology shall be applied in the following order: Voluntary Downward Movement, Involuntary Downward Movement, Movement Within Classification (Voluntary and Involuntary), and Voluntary Upward Movement.

V. INVOLUNTARY DOWNWARD MOVEMENT [*sample of movement methodology*]

C. Employees who are involuntarily downgraded shall be assigned a new Job Status in accordance with their Involuntary Downward Movement choices, Seniority, and the following sequence of steps for each choice, starting with the first choice:

1. Step 1: The employee shall first be assigned to an existing Opening which matches the indicated choice.
2. Step 2: If the employee cannot be moved in Step 1, then the employee shall be assigned to an existing Opening, created by a Level One Volunteer, which matches the indicated choice.
3. Step 3: If the employee cannot be moved in Step 2, then the employee shall be assigned to an existing Opening, created by a Level Two Volunteer, which matches the indicated choice.

* * * *

8. Step 8: If the employee cannot be moved to an Opening in Step 7, above, then the employee shall be displaced from the Seniority Unit.

D. Employees who are bumped under C., 4., above, shall be assigned a new Job Status in accordance with their Involuntary Movement Within Classification choices, Seniority, and the following sequence of steps for each choice, starting with the first choice:

* * * *

E. Employees who are bumped under D., 3., above, shall be assigned to a new Job Status in accordance with their Involuntary Movement Within Classification choices, Seniority, and the following sequences of steps, for each choice, starting with the first choice:

* * * *

F. Employees who are bumped under E.,3., above. . . .
* * * *

VII. VOLUNTARY UPWARD MOVEMENT
   A. Employees may indicate their desired Voluntary Upward Movement choices on their Job Preference Sheets. . . .
   B. Openings in the Labor Pool, which remain after Preference Movement has taken place, shall be filled by those employees possessing the greatest Company Seniority among qualified employees in other Seniority Units who have submitted an appropriate request in accordance with the conditions of Supplemental Agreement E. . . .
   C. Openings in Classifications above the Labor Pool, which remain after Preference Movement has taken place, shall be filled by the most senior qualified employees in the next lower Classification in the Line of Progression or in the Labor Pool, whose indicated choices, starting with the highest choice, match the existing Opening. . . .
   D. If Openings in Lines of Progression remain after completing C., above, then the Company shall post the Opening to the entire Seniority Unit for five (5) working days. . . .

Supplemental Agreement E
Voluntary Transfers Between Seniority Units

PURPOSE

In order to provide some flexibility to employees, while maintaining stability of the work forces in the various Seniority Units, the Company and the Union are agreed to the following principles whereby employees can be transferred, at their request, from one Seniority Unit to another.
   I. Employees requesting transfer from one Seniority Unit to another shall do so in writing with a copy of the request to be given to their supervisor and duly authorized Shop Representative.
* * * *
   V. No employee with less than one (1) year of Company seniority shall be considered eligible for transfer between Seniority Units in accordance with provision to this Supplemental Agreement unless otherwise agreed to in each individual case by the Company and the Union.
* * * *
  VII. In any calendar year, no more than ten percent (10%) of the employees of any one Seniority Unit shall be transferred out of that Seniority Unit.
* * * *
  IX. Employees shall not be eligible to transfer under the terms of this Supplemental Agreement more often than once.

Schedule H
Profit Sharing Plan

I. PARTICIPATION IN THE PLAN

Employees participate in the plan, in accordance with the following schedule of their length of service with the Company, as of December 31 of the calendar year on which the profit sharing contribution is based:

Length of Service	Participation
Less than 6 months	None
6 months, but less than 2 years	85%
2 years but less than 3 years	90%
3 years or more	100%

II. DETERMINATION OF AMOUNT OF PROFIT SHARING CONTRIBUTION

A. The money set aside for profit sharing comes from the consolidated income of the Company.

B. The amount of the profit sharing contribution is based on a ratio of consolidated income before taxes to the Company's average total assets. The resulting percentage is called "Return on Assets."

C. The profit sharing contribution for each year is based on an employee's reported annual W-2 earnings in that year, excluding the previous year's profit sharing contribution, occasional absence payments, tuition aid payments, and relocation allowances.

D. The profit sharing contribution is allocated between a Retirement Account and Profit Sharing Savings Account. The following table is a summary of the allocation:

Return on Assets	Retirement Account	Profit Sharing Savings Account
11.5% or less	5.00	0.00
12	5.00	0.40
13	5.00	1.30
14	5.00	2.20
15	5.30	2.80
16	5.75	3.25
17	6.15	3.65
18	6.55	4.05
19	6.95	4.45
20	7.35	4.85
21	7.75	5.25
22	8.15	5.65
23	8.55	6.05
23.5 or more	8.75	6.25

E. The minimum profit sharing contribution is five (5%) percent of pay, regardless of the "Return on Assets."

Supplemental Agreement J
Job Evaluation Agreement

III. DESCRIPTION AND CLASSIFICATION OF JOBS

A. Joint Job Evaluation Committee

A Joint Job Evaluation Committee hereinafter referred to as "the Committee" is established for the purpose of assigning jobs into a proper labor grade based on study and evaluation of job content.

1. The Union shall be represented on the Committee by six (6) members selected by the Union so as to be representative of the various Seniority Units. One of these six (6) Union members on the Committee shall be the National Director, Xerographic Division, A.C.T.W.U., AFL-CIO, or the Director's designated representative.

2. The Company shall be represented on the Committee by six (6) members selected by the Company so as to be representative of the various manufacturing operations. One of these six (6) Company members on the Committee shall be a representative from Corporate Industrial Relations.

* * * *

8. In cases where unanimous agreement among Committee members cannot be attained relative to the assignment of a job to a labor grade, a fact-finding subcommittee of four (4) Committee members, two (2) Union representatives and two (2) Company representatives, shall be appointed by the Committee Co-Chairpersons to report their findings of facts and recommendations related thereto. . . .

C. Changes in Existing Jobs
1. When the Company changes, in a significant manner, the job content (job requirements as to skill, responsibility, effort, and working conditions) of an existing job, the Company shall record the changes involved on a Job Description and Job Rating form showing additions to or deletions from the job description.

Supplemental Agreement K
Fabrication Department Agreement on Subcontracting

The Company and Union agree to the following terms relative to the Webster Fabrication Department.

I. WORK JURISDICTION

The work jurisdiction of the Fabrication Department shall include the following:

A. Volume production work in the established Commodity Codes (listed at end of this Supplemental Agreement) as listed below:
1. Parts for finished products made in Rochester when the Company already has the manufacturing physical plant, tools, and equipment to fabricate or produce such parts.
2. Spare parts for products which are or have been made in Rochester.
3. Parts made for Xerox products not made in Rochester.
4. Temporary runs of parts which ultimately will be fabricated in other countries.
5. Parts made under contract which are not used in Xerox products.
6. Parts made for Xerox products manufactured in Xerox plants in other countries in accordance with projected Export-Import Balancing Agreements.

B. The production of Xerox proprietary parts which are not included in the established Commodity Codes, e.g., fuser rolls and turned drum blanks.

C. The Short-Run Shop.

D. The Tool Room.

II. EXCLUSIONS

The work jurisdiction of the Fabrication Department shall exclude the following:

A. Work which is not included in the established Commodity Codes, as well as the work once in Commodity Codes which themselves no longer exist.

B. Parts of "Old Generation" products (the Xerox 914 and 813 copier families) which will be discontinued from production schedules.

C. Parts for Xerox products manufactured in Xerox plants in other countries which may be excluded from production by the Fabrication Department in accordance with projected Export-Import Balancing Agreements.

D. Parts which are appropriate in the work jurisdiction of other Bargaining Units.

Commodity Codes Descriptions

203 *Large Sheet Metal:* including bases, frames, housings, chassis and supports, large panels, covers, etc.—over 150 through 800 ton punch press required.

301 *Small Short Turned Parts:* very simple, one screw machine operations required.

303 *Long Turned Parts:* including shafts over 8" long, tie rods, rollers, etc.

405 *Casting:* Large size, complex; complexity of the parts requires boring and accurate milling, or more than two planes.

100 *Welding:* Contains "S" numbered parts that do not qualify for 200, 300, 400, or 700 commodity classifications.

500 *Mechanical Assemblies:* Contains only "S" numbered parts whose routings fail all other commodity tests.

202 *Medium Sheet Metal:* including chutes, paper trays, transports, rails, plates, brackets and paper guides—over 60 through 100 ton press required.

403 *Casting:* Medium size, complex. Requires accurate milling.

302 *Small Short Turned Parts:* More complex than 301—one screw machine and mill and/or drill operations required.

401 *Casting:* Small simple—may have one mill or one drill operation.

201 *Small Sheet Metal:* including assorted brackets, levers, stiffeners, clamps, clips, and buckets—through 80 ton punch press required.

The Construction Industry: Four Decades of Public Policy Debate

In July 1984, H.R. 6043, the Construction Industry Labor Law Amendments of 1984 was introduced to the House of Representatives by Congressman Clay, but received no legislative consideration during the balance of the 98th Congress.

On January 3, 1985, Clay reintroduced the bill as H.R. 281. On April 17, 1986, the House of Representatives passed the bill by a vote of 229 to 173. The companion Senate bill, S. 2181, however, never received consideration during the 99th Congress.

H.R. 281, the Building and Construction Industry Labor Law Amendments of 1987, was again introduced in the House of Representatives on January 6, 1987 (see Exhibit 1, p. 191). On June 17, 1987, the bill again passed the House and was again sent to the Senate, where a companion bill, S. 492, had been introduced on February 7, 1987. The bill passed the Senate Labor Committee in early December; the committee report was being written in early 1988; and the bill was expected to be on the Senate floor in spring 1988.

THE CONSTRUCTION INDUSTRY

Two major segments, public and private, comprise the $400 billion construction and building industry (see Exhibit 2, p. 194). Beyond this preliminary segmentation, private construction is either residential or nonresidential (see Exhibit 3, p. 194); and public construction is further segmented as either state and local versus federal, buildings or non-buildings projects (Exhibit 4, see p. 195). Total annual volume varies greatly state to state, depending upon business development, population growth, and award of federally funded projects (see Exhibit 5, p. 195). In all locales, however, the industry tends to be seasonal, with the largest construction volume occurring during the spring and summer months even in those parts of the country with mild climates.

In addition to being cyclical, the construction industry is also characterized by a transient, highly skilled labor force that moves in waves through projects at varying stages of completion. For example, construction of a typical residential home entails numerous steps: clearing the lot, digging footings and other foundation work; connecting water and sewer lines; laying slab and/or brick blocks; framing the walls and roof; duct work; electrical rough-in; insulation; preliminary lath work or drywall; completing the roof; tiling, priming; installing windows and doors; installing heating/air conditioning equipment; interior finish work and cabinetry; electrical trim; wallpapering and decorating; cleaning house, grading yard; inspection; and landscaping. The process flows smoothly provided the necessary workers are available at the time they are needed. This is critical, as most contractors on construction projects are heavily penalized on a per diem basis for delayed completion.

In response to the need for readily available, highly skilled workers, the industry traditionally relied upon union workers available through union hiring halls (Exhibit 6, see p. 197). Signatory to a labor agreement, termed "prehire agreements," contractors bid on jobs knowing the prevailing wage rate for each step in the project. Contractors maintained access to trained workers through the hiring hall referral system on an as-needed basis, eliminating the need for a permanent payroll. As trade unions maintain their own extensive apprenticeship training programs, contractors have foregone the burden of screening employees. While this system addressed industry-specific needs, prehire agreements were technically illegal under the National Labor Relations Act until remedial legislation was passed in 1959.

CONSTRUCTION INDUSTRY LEGISLATIVE HISTORY

In 1935, the Wagner Act (National Labor Relations Act) set forth the time-consuming election requirements necessary for a union to claim representation rights of a bargaining unit. Although the Wagner Act did not specifically exclude jurisdiction over the construction industry, which, due to the transient nature of the work force, would find it difficult to comply with election requirements, the National Labor Relations Board (NLRB) refused to assert any jurisdiction in construction-related cases.

The 1947 Taft-Hartley Act (Labor Management Relations Act), however, brought the construction industry within the Act's jurisdiction. Under Taft-Hartley, contractors who signed union contracts before employees were hired would be considered in violation of Section 8(a)(3) for unlawful discrimination in favor of the union; unions insisting on such prehire contracts would be found in violation of Section 8(b)(2).

A series of NLRB decisions complying with Taft-Hartley resulted in sufficient uproar from both contractors and the trade unions that Congress enacted Section 8(f) in the Landrum-Griffin Act of 1959, which states:

> It shall not be an unfair labor practice under subsections (a) and (b) of this section for an employer engaged primarily in the building and construction industry to make an agreement covering employees engaged (or who, upon their employment, will be engaged) in the building and construction industry with a labor organization of which building and construction employees are members (not established, maintained, or assisted by an action defined in section 8(a) of this Act as an unfair labor practice) because (1) the majority status of such labor organization has not been established under the provisions of section 9 of this Act prior to the making of such agreement, or (2) such agreement requires as a condition of employment, membership in such labor organization after the seventh day following the beginning of such employment or the effective date of the agreement, whichever is later, or (3) such agreement requires the employer to notify such labor organization of opportunities for employment with such employer, or gives such labor organization an opportunity to refer qualified applicants for such employment, or (4) such agreement specifies minimum training or experience qualifications for employment or provides for priority in opportunities for employment based upon length of service with such employer, in the industry or in the particular geographical area; *Provided,* That nothing in this subsection shall set aside the final proviso to section 8(a)(3)* of the Act: *Provided further,* That any agreement which would be invalid, but for clause (1) of this subsection, shall not be a bar to a petition filed pursuant to section 9(c) or 9(e).[1]

---

*This being: "That no employer shall justify any discrimination against an employee for nonmembership in a labor organization (A) if he has reasonable grounds for believing that such membership was not available to the employee on the same terms and conditions generally applicable to other members, or (B) if he has reasonable grounds for believing that membership was denied or terminated for reasons other than the failure of the employee to tender the periodic dues and the initiation fees uniformly required as a condition of acquiring or retaining membership."

Subsequent NLRB and court decisions, however, focused on the two provisos of Section 8(f), giving a more limited definition and scope to prehire agreements as collective bargaining agreements under the Act. In particular, the Board's 1971 *R.J. Smith Construction Company* decision

---

[1]Section 9(c) pertains to requirements for certification elections, whereas Section 9(e) pertains to employees' right to decertify a union.

and the Supreme Court's 1978 *NLRB* v. *Iron Workers Local 103 (Higdon Contracting Company)* decision ruled that Section 8(f) agreements fall short of Section 9(a) agreements in that, unlike traditional collective bargaining agreements, 8(f) agreements are voidable at any time by either party.

In *R.J. Smith*, the Board ruled that 8(f) agreements were only "a preliminary step that contemplates further action for the development of a full bargaining relationship." As a preliminary step, the Board held that 8(f) agreements confer no presumption of majority status, and thus the union's status as the workers' collective bargaining representative could be challenged at any time during the contract term. Further, a signatory employer could test the union's majority status by repudiating the 8(f) agreement and litigating through an 8(a)(5) proceeding.

The *R.J. Smith* decision, however, also introduced the "conversion doctrine," allowing that an 8(f) relationship could convert to a full 9(a) collective bargaining relationship upon (1) a showing that the union did enjoy majority support, (2) during the relevant period, (3) among an appropriate bargaining unit of a signatory employer's employees.

A union could prove majority support in numerous ways: the presence within the 8(f) agreement of a union-security clause, the union membership of a majority of unit employees, lists of referrals from the hiring hall, or employer contributions to a union-administered fringe benefit fund were all considered evidentiary of union majority status.

The relevant period was not the time an 8(f) agreement was repudiated; based upon a 1982 Board decision, "The relevant period for a meaningful showing of majority support is normally within the effective term of the applicable collective bargaining agreement." Within other Board decisions, however, the relevant period ranged greatly. The 1975 *Wheeler Construction Company* decision ruled that at the time of adoption of the 8(f) agreement, the signatory union enjoyed majority support among the bargaining unit. Conversely, in the 1981 *Carrothers Construction Company* decision, the Board ruled that a 1976 8(f) agreement repudiation was unlawful based upon a 1966 showing of majority support.

In determining an appropriate bargaining unit, the Board distinguished between single employers and multiemployers. For a single employer, the Board delineated between a permanent and stable work force versus a project-by-project work force. Within a permanent and stable work force, that entire work force was the appropriate bargaining unit for majority-status determination. Within a project-by-project work force, the Board required majority proof on each individual project, with status not transferable between projects. If a single employer joined a multiemployer bargaining group, the single employer's unit merged into the larger unit, with majority support necessary within the entire multiemployer unit. For multiemployers, the Board did not distinguish unit determination by the nature of the work.

Once conversion occurred, the 8(f) union acquired immediate 9(a) status, and an employer was under the statutory duty to recognize and bargain with the union as the employees' exclusive representative.

The 1978 Supreme Court *Higdon* decision upheld the Board's interpretation of 8(f) agreements, stating that the interpretation was "acceptable, but not the only tenable one." Further, the Court determined that workers could not picket an employer for violating an 8(f) agreement. The Court found that Section 8(b)(7)(C) of the Labor Management Relations Act ensured voluntary, uncoerced employee selection of a bargaining unit representative. As an 8(f) agreement does not require a showing of majority status, the Court ruled that, "[Absent] majority credentials . . . the collective-bargaining relationship and the union's entitlement to act as the exclusive bargaining agent had never matured. Picketing to enforce the Section 8(f) contract was the legal equivalent of picketing to require recognition as the exclusive agent, and Section 8(b)(7)(C) was infringed when the union failed to request an election within 30 days."

RECENT INDUSTRY CHANGES

During the time the Board and courts applied and interpreted Section 8(f), a shift occurred within construction industry employment. As inflation slowed new construction, cost-containment pressures increased the popularity of the nonunion merit shop.

In addition to wage differentials between union and nonunion construction workers, unions contend that nonunion workers lack sufficient skills training. Within the United Brotherhood of Carpenters, four years are required to become a journeyman carpenter. Similar training within merit shops is typically 90 days. Unions claim that the additional training increases worker productivity due to greater knowledge and less supervision. Research supports this claim, but only in certain settings.[2] Merit shop supporters argue that unions force contractors to use more skilled workers (in place of semiskilled workers) than required.

Despite claims of lower productivity, by 1986 merit shops garnered more than half of all annual construction volume, and annual wage increases slowed (see Exhibit 7, p. 198). Nonunion strength, however, is not uniform throughout the industry. Merit shops prevail in residential construction, whereas unions maintain strength in commercial, industrial, and federally assisted projects subject to prevailing wage rates

---

[2]For example, see Steven G. Allen, "Unionization and Productivity in Office Building and School Construction," *Industrial & Labor Relations Review* 39, no. 2 (January 1986) pp. 187–201.

under the Davis-Bacon Act. (Exhibit 8 depicts employment among the different types of construction, see p. 199).

Because different types of construction projects are bid among either predominantly union or predominantly nonunion competition, an increasing number of employers become double breasted. Under these configurations, employers maintain one construction company signatory to an 8(f) agreement, and open a second, nonunion company to take advantage of those markets where competition is predominantly nonunion. However, during periods of high unemployment in the construction industry, some union members work at nonunion job sites for nonunion wages.

A REVERSAL IN BOARD LAW

Shortly after H.R. 281 was introduced during the 100th Congress, the NLRB issued the *John Deklewa & Sons* decision. In June 1960 John Deklewa & Sons entered into a prehire agreement with Iron Workers, Local 3. Twenty years later, the company joined the Iron Workers Employer Association of Western Pennsylvania, which executed a bargaining agreement with Local 3 effective 1982 through 1985. Under the terms of the agreement, the company relied exclusively on the hiring hall for its ironworkers on three projects running from June 1982 through April 1983.

On September 21, 1983, John Deklewa & Sons resigned from the multiemployer association and also repudiated their prehire agreement with Local 3. By a letter dated September 27, the union objected to the company's repudiation of the agreement and withdrawal of recognition. Three days later, the union filed a grievance that the company was violating the subcontracting clause of the 1982–85 agreement at a project that began September 7 (and ultimately was to run through December 14). The company responded that the dispute was not arbitrable as they had repudiated the agreement and were no longer bound by its provisions.

In reviewing the case, the Board decided to reconsider its earlier decisions regarding 8(f) agreements. Although *Higdon* provided a Supreme Court ruling supporting the current Board law, the Board noted that the Court had ruled that, "the Board's construction of the Act, although perhaps not the only tenable one, is an acceptable reading of the statutory language." The Board argued that a more tenable interpretation would eliminate serious shortcomings of the current law:

> First, the current law does not fully square with either Section 8(f)'s legislative history or that section's actual wording. Second, the current law inadequately serves the fundamental statutory objectives of employee free choice and labor relations stability. Third, the frustration of statutory policies is increased be-

cause of the administrative and litigational difficulties created by the current law. Accordingly, we find it both necessary and appropriate to abandon the Board's existing interpretation of Section 8(f).

We find that this law now often operates in a manner that contradicts the apparent congressional intent. . . . There is no express language in the legislative history of the text of the Act declaring a congressional view that such collective bargaining agreements, specifically authorized by the Act, are nonbinding, unenforceable, or subject to repudiation at will. . . . If the legislative history and statutory language discussed above indicate anything, it is an intent by Congress to legitimate and make enforceable the array of construction industry bargaining, referral, hiring, and employment practices that the Board had previously found to be unlawful, and thus unenforceable under the Act. . . . Because . . . a right of unilateral repudiation is so antithetical to traditional principles of collective bargaining under the Act, it seems likely that Congress would have expressly stated such a right if it intended to create one. . . .

Congress was concerned, however, about employees' ability to rid themselves of an existing representative, or select an alternate one, once the 8(f) relationship was fully established. Thus, Congress specified that an 8(f) agreement may not act as a bar to, inter alia, decertification or rival union petitions.

Although the aforementioned legislative history indicates certain assumptions about a union's ability to achieve majority support after executing an 8(f) agreement, the legislative history and statutory language are devoid by an indication that Congress contemplated the extraordinary "conversion" of such nonbinding relationships into full-fledged, wholly enforceable 9(a) relationships constituting an absolute bar to employees' efforts to reject or to change their collective bargaining representative. In our view, this particular aspect of the conversion doctrine contravenes Congress' intent to provide employees with a meaningful and readily available escape hatch.

Finally, the current 8(f) unit determination rules likewise fail to reflect the objectives Congress expressed in enacting Section 8(f). First, current law draws a sharp distinction between "permanent and stable" and "project-by-project" work forces. Yet, Congress described the construction industry generally as one that hires employees on a project-by-project basis. That very characteristic was one of the underlying reasons for Section 8(f)'s enactment. The Board's artificial bifurcation of the industry along these lines, therefore, seems plainly contrary to Congress' expressed view of the industry. Second, to the extent current law applies the merger doctrine to Section 8(f), and thereby renders practically insignificant the representational desires of a single employer's employees in multiemployer associations, it places an additional obstacle in the way of employees who wish to reject or change their collective bargaining representative.

In criticizing current Board law vis-à-vis the goals of employee free choice and labor relations stability, the Board argued that the conversion doctrine inhibited employee free choice by creating "an irrebuttable majority presumption during the contract term," with any election petition thereby being barred by the Board's contract-bar rules. Such a situation, according to the Board, completely negated the intent of the second proviso of Section 8(f). Moreover, the Board contended that "a rule that sanctions unilateral contract repudiation and the inevitable disruptions that result is not conducive to labor relations stability."

Finally, the Board criticized the evidentiary determinations to be "inexact, impractical, and generally insufficient to support the conclusions they purport to demonstrate." In light of these factors, the Board went on to decide: "Accordingly, we overrule *R.J. Smith, Dee Cee Floor Covering, Authorized Air Conditioning,* and their progeny to the extent inconsistent with this decision, and we shall no longer apply the so-called conversion doctrine to 8(f) cases."

After considerable written discussion regarding appropriate alternative law, the Board determined that:

> We shall apply the following principles in 8(f) cases: (1) a collective bargaining agreement permitted by Section 8(f) shall be enforceable through the mechanisms of Section 8(a)(5) and Section 8(b)(3); (2) such agreements will not bar the processing of valid petitions filed pursuant to Section 9(c) and Section 9(e); (3) in processing such petitions, the appropriate unit normally will be the single employer's employees covered by the agreement; and (4) upon the expiration of such agreements, the signatory union will enjoy no presumption of majority status, and either party may repudiate the 8(f) bargaining relationship.

The Board's decision is under appeal.

THE BUILDING AND CONSTRUCTION INDUSTRY LABOR LAW AMENDMENTS OF 1987

Supporters of H.R. 281 claim the amendments are necessary in light of Board and court interpretations of the 1959 amendments.

> One line of cases has allowed construction industry management to sign collective bargaining agreements and to then ignore those agreements through the simple device of establishing other companies to do the same work in the same area under nonunion conditions as often as is necessary to defeat the right to organize [i.e., *Peter Kiewit,* 206 NLRB 562 (1973)]. The other series of decisions permitted construction industry management to repudiate Section 8(f) collective bargaining agreements and terminate their bargaining relationship at will. Both of these devices—which are endemic only in the construction industry—are contrary to the most elementary notions of good faith dealing that should be the hallmark of contractual relationships generally and of collective bargaining relationships particularly. (citations added)[3]

Bill supporters argued that *Deklewa* did not fully resolve construction industry labor difficulties, and that portions of the decision actually

---

[3]House of Representatives Report 100–137: *Dissenting Views and Supplemental Dissenting Views,* [To accompany H.R. 281], June 8, 1987, p. 6.

furthered the need for remedial legislation. First, while *Deklewa* somewhat amends previous prehire agreement precedence, the decision does not address the issue of double-breasted employers. Second, while

> The Board's *Deklewa* decision is responsive to the criticism directed at its . . . line of cases . . . [i]n other respects . . . however, the *Deklewa* decision is extremely troubling and unsettling and fails to recognize the full import of congressional intent in 1959. While the Board held in *Deklewa* that a prehire agreement may not be repudiated during its term, it also held that the moment that the prehire agreement expires, the employer has no continuing duty even to bargain with the union. There is no continuing presumption of the union's majority support (as there is in other industries). . . . Moreover, every collective bargaining agreement in the construction industry will be assumed to be a prehire agreement unless it is actually proved to be a Section 9(a) collective bargaining agreement.[4]

Supporters were also concerned about the Board's rejection of evidence which had previously been acceptable for a showing of majority support, such as when a majority of employees were indeed union members. Further, *Deklewa* disallowed a construction industry union's use of economic pressure to compel employers to bargain for a new agreement, since recognitional picketing was limited to 30 days. Thus H.R. 281 supporters argued that amendments should be added, resulting in the version depicted in the Appendix (page 200).

Opposition to H.R. 281 claimed that, "its implications have been vastly oversimplified leading to widespread misunderstanding about both the current situation and the ultimate effects of the bill."[5] Opponents recognized the pre-*Deklewa* flaws of being able to repudiate prehire agreements and found the decision satisfactory regarding contract term provisions:

> It should be noted that, in other industries, there is usually a continuing bargaining obligation in "section 9(a) cases" where a union has been formally certified by the Board as the majority representative of the employees. The rule in *Deklewa* is consistent with that general rule. However, H.R. 281 would require a continuing bargaining obligation upon expiration of the contract even though the majority status may never have been demonstrated.[6]

So while opponents to H.R. 281 agreed that employers should not be able to freely abrogate prehire agreements, they claimed the Board's *Deklewa* decision provided a "better balance between the Act's goals of protecting employee free choice and promoting labor stability."[7]

Opponents also objected to the double-breasting provisions of the proposed bill for two reasons. First, they claimed the bill would impose

---

[4]Ibid., p. 9.
[5]Ibid., p. 18.
[6]Ibid., p. 19.
[7]Ibid., p. 19.

union representation upon workers, eliminating their freedom of choice for representation. As the 1959 amendments were enacted due to difficulties in organizing the project-by-project work forces, opponents felt this same shortcoming applied to organizing decertification elections. Thus, employees would have union representation forced upon them with little practical recourse under Section 9 of the Act. Conversely, opponents argued, such a provision would encourage most employers to go nonunion, thereby eliminating employees' choice *of* union representation.

The second criticism of H.R. 281's antidouble-breasting provisions pointed that the alter ego doctrine already forbade the setting up of a new company for no other reason than to avoid an existing collective bargaining agreement. Beyond this, construction industry employers had legitimate interests given the market segmentation in maintaining double-breasted operations, without any loss of employment to the union shop:

> The point is that frequently the use of an open shop company versus a union shop company is pre-ordinated because of forces beyond the control of the double-breasted companies. This was recently described by the General Counsel for the National Labor Relations Board in a brief to the Board in the *Manganaro* case . . . which involves double-breasted drywall contractors in the Washington, D.C., area: "[A]n examination of the record evidence reveals . . . that the overwhelming number of projects are bid exclusively by either union only or nonunion drywall contractors. . . . Moreover, the rare circumstances in which union and nonunion contractors submit bids for the same project occur so infrequently that they cannot be said to obliterate the general rule."[8]

Thus, opponents believed that abandoning the distinction between legitimate and abusive double-breasting as proposed within H.R. 281 would ultimately destabilize labor within the construction industry.

On June 17, 1987, H.R. 281 passed by a vote of 227 to 197.

QUESTION

As a member of the Senate, do you believe the companion bill S. 492 should be passed and the Amendments become law?

---

[8]Ibid., p. 21.

EXHIBIT 1

100TH CONGRESS **H. R. 281**
1ST SESSION

To amend the National Labor Relations Act to increase the stability of collective bargaining in the building and construction industry.

IN THE HOUSE OF REPRESENTATIVES

JANUARY 6, 1987

Mr. CLAY introduced the following bill; which referred to the Committee on Education and Labor

---

A BILL

To amend the National Labor Relations Act to increase the stability of collective bargaining in the building and construction industry.

1   *Be it enacted by the Senate and House of Representa-*

2 *tives of the United States of America in Congress assembled,*

3 That this Act may be referred to as the "Construction Indus-

4 try Labor Law Amendments of 1985".

5   SEC. 2 (a) Section 2(2) of the National Labor Relations

6 Act (29 U.S.C. 152(2)) is amended by adding at the end

7 thereof the following new sentence: "In the construction in-

8 dustry, any two or more business entities performing or oth-

9 erwise conducting or supervising the same or similar work,

EXHIBIT 1—*Continued*

2

1 in the same or in different geographical areas, and having,

2 directly or indirectly—

3   "(a) substantial common ownership;

4   "(b) common management; or

5   "(c) common control;

6 shall be deemed a single employer.".

7   (b) Section 8(d) of such Act (29 U.S.C. 158(d)) is

8 amended by adding at the end thereof the following new

9 sentence: "Whenever the collective bargaining involves em-

10 ployees of a business entity comprising part of a single em-

11 ployer in the construction industry, as defined in section 2(2)

12 of this Act, the duty to bargain collectively, for the purposes

13 of this section, shall include the duty to apply the terms of a

14 collective bargaining agreement between such business entity

15 and a labor organization to all other business entities com-

16 prising the single employer within the geographical area cov-

17 ered by the agreement.".

18   (c) Section 8(f) of such Act (29 U.S.C. 158(f)) is

19 amended—

20   (1) by striking out "geographical area:" in clause

21   (4) and inserting in lieu thereof the following: "geo-

22   graphic area. An agreement lawfully made pursuant to

23   this subsection shall impose the same obligations under

24   this Act as an agreement made with a majority repre-

25   sentative pursuant to section 9(a):"; and

EXHIBIT 1—*Concluded*

3

1   (2) by inserting before the period at the end of

2   such section and the following new proviso: "*: Pro-*

3   *vided further,* That any agreement lawfully made pur-

4   suant to this subsection may be repudiated only after

5   the Board certifies the results of an election conducted

6   pursuant to section 9(c), in which a majority of em-

7   ployees in an appropriate bargaining unit selects a bar-

8   gaining representative other than the labor organiza-

9   tion with which such agreement was made or chooses

10   not to be represented by a labor organization".

11   SEC. 3. (a) Except as provided in subsection (b), the

12   amendments made by section 2 shall take effect upon the

13   date of the enactment of this Act.

14   (b) The requirement imposed by the amendment made

15   by section 2(b) shall take effect—

16   (1) one year after such date of enactment with re-

17   spect to any building and construction project for

18   which the contract was entered into by an employer

19   before the date of the enactment of this Act; and

20   (2) on the date on which the contract is entered

21   into with respect to any new building or construction

22   project for which the contract is entered into by an

23   employer on or after the date of the enactment of this

24   Act.

EXHIBIT 2 Annual Value of New Construction, 1977–1986 (billions of dollars)

Type	1977	1978	1979	1980	1981	1982	1983	1984	1985	1986
Private construction										
Residential	92	110	116	100	99	85	126	154	158	187
Nonresidential	30	38	50	55	65	69	66	81	95	91
Public utilities	21	25	28	31	34	34	32	31	33	34
All other	1	1	1	1	1	1	1	2	3	2
Public construction										
Buildings	13	15	16	19	18	17	17	18	20	24
Highways and streets	11	13	15	17	17	16	17	19	22	23
Sewer and water	7	9	12	10	9	8	7	8	10	11
Conservation	4	4	5	5	5	5	5	5	5	5
Military	1	2	2	2	2	2	3	3	3	4
Miscellaneous public	4	5	5	5	6	5	5	5	5	5

Source: U.S. Department of Commerce.

EXHIBIT 3 Private Construction by Type, 1982–1986 (billions of dollars)

Type	1982	1983	1984	1985	1986
Residential					
One unit	41.5	72.2	85.6	86.1	102.2
Two units or more	15.5	22.4	28.2	28.5	31.0
Improvements	27.7	30.9	40.0	43.8	54.0
Nonresidential					
Industrial buildings	6.1	5.8	9.1	9.5	9.7
Office buildings	12.9	12.6	16.0	18.1	14.4
Service stations/garages	.2	.3	.4	.5	.5
Stores and mercantile	5.5	7.4	9.8	12.0	12.1
Religious buildings	.9	1.0	1.1	1.2	1.4
Educational buildings	1.0	1.0	1.0	1.3	1.3
Hospitals and institutions	2.0	2.4	2.0	2.5	2.6
Amusement buildings	.7	.8	.8	.9	1.1
Residential garages	.8	1.0	1.0	1.2	1.3
Other buildings	3.1	3.0	3.4	4.5	3.9
Other structures	1.4	1.7	1.9	2.1	2.2

Source: U.S. Department of Commerce.

EXHIBIT 4   Public Construction by Type, 1982–1986 (billions of dollars)

Type	1982	1983	1984	1985	1986
State and local					
Educational	5.4	5.0	5.9	6.7	8.4
Hospitals	1.3	1.4	.9	1.1	1.1
Other buildings	7.2	6.1	7.3	8.9	8.7
Highways and streets	13.0	15.6	16.7	21.5	23.0
Sewer and water facilities	7.8	8.2	8.7	11.2	12.5
Other nonbuildings	3.5	4.5	4.3	5.6	5.0
Federal					
Housekeeping residences	.1	.3	.3	.2	.3
Educational	.1	.2	.2	.3	.3
Hospitals and institutions	.6	.6	.5	.6	.8
Administrative/service	.4	.9	.7	1.0	1.3
Airfield-related	.3	.5	.4	.6	.8
Troop housing	.2	.2	.3	.4	.4
Warehouses	.1	.1	.1	.2	.3
Conservation	1.3	1.1	1.0	.9	.9
Highways and streets	.3	.4	.3	.3	.2
Electric power	.2	.4	.1	.3	.3
All other	1.5	1.5	1.5	2.2	2.2

Source: U.S. Department of Commerce, Bureau of the Census.

EXHIBIT 5   Private Construction by State, 1986

State	Nonresidential (millions of dollars)	Residential (number of units)
Alabama*†	$ 837	19,180
Alaska	143	1,353
Arizona*†	1,623	61,614
Arkansas	378	8,719
California	11,814	314,641
Colorado†	1,116	30,961
Connecticut	1,173	27,730
Delaware	269	5,527
D.C.	181	640
Florida*†	5,045	195,525
Georgia*†	2,478	76,896
Hawaii	326	7,217
Idaho*†	172	3,804
Illinois	2,974	51,876
Indiana	1,306	29,686
Iowa*†	408	5,472

EXHIBIT 5—*Concluded*

State	Nonresidential (millions of dollars)	Residential (number of units)
Kansas*†	656	13,086
Kentucky	541	13,503
Louisiana*	863	10,501
Maine	367	9,554
Maryland	1,826	42,378
Massachusetts	2,215	45,215
Michigan	2,652	47,230
Minnesota	1,576	33,215
Mississippi*†	413	8,289
Missouri	1,407	33,208
Montana	79	1,153
Nebraska*	247	6,236
Nevada*	593	15,655
New Hampshire†	414	18,015
New Jersey	2,212	57,352
New Mexico	356	11,513
New York	2,849	60,198
North Carolina*†	2,014	62,995
North Dakota*†	81	1,702
Ohio	2,444	44,460
Oklahoma	419	8,984
Oregon	591	10,662
Pennsylvania	2,746	53,442
Rhode Island	165	7,274
South Carolina*†	962	26,840
South Dakota*†	106	1,981
Tennessee*	1,285	34,356
Texas*	5,262	96,737
Utah*†	523	13,827
Vermont†	172	4,478
Virginia*†	2,571	73,511
Washington	1,437	36,434
West Virginia	151	1,918
Wisconsin	1,102	21,824
Wyoming*	192	876

*Right-to-work state.
†State without a state prevailing wage rate.

Source: U.S. Department of Commerce, U.S. Department of Labor, Bureau of Labor Statistics.

EXHIBIT 6 Construction Industry—Labor Unions

Union	1987 Membership*
Aluminum, Brick and Glass Workers	45,000
International Association of Bridge, Structural and Ornamental Iron Workers	122,000
International Association of Heat and Frost Insulators and Asbestos Workers	12,000
International Brotherhood of Boilermakers, Iron Shipbuilders, Blacksmiths, Forgers and Helpers (including United Cement, Lime, Gypsum and Allied Workers Division)	90,000
International Brotherhood of Electrical Workers	765,000
International Brotherhood of Painters and Allied Trades	128,000
International Brotherhood of Teamsters, Chauffeurs, Warehousemen and Helpers of America	1,800,000
International Federation of Professional and Technical Engineers	20,000
International Union of Bricklayers and Allied Craftsmen	84,000
International Union of Elevator Constructors	21,000
International Union of Operating Engineers	330,000
International Woodworkers of America	26,000
Laborers' International Union of North America	371,000
Metal Polishers, Buffers, Platers and Allied Workers International Union	5,000
Operative Plasterers' and Cement Masons' International Association	43,000
Sheet Metal Workers' International Association	108,000
Stove, Furnace and Allied Appliance Workers' International Union of North America	3,000
Tile, Marble, Terrazzo, Finishers, Shopworkers and Granite Cutters International Union	8,000
United Association of Journeymen and Apprentices of the Plumbing and Pipe Fitting Industry of the U.S. and Canada	220,000
United Brotherhood of Carpenters and Joiners of America	609,000
United Rubber, Cork, Linoleum and Plastic Workers of America	97,000
United Steelworkers of America	494,000
United Union of Roofers, Waterproofers and Allied Workers	25,000

*Average of the two-year period ending June 30, 1987.

Source: 1987 Report of the AFL-CIO Executive Committee; and the Int'l Brotherhood of Teamsters Communications Dept.

EXHIBIT 7 Construction Industry—1977–1986 Employment Statistics

Year	Total Employees	Workers	Average Hourly Earnings	Average Weekly Hours
1977	3,851,000	3,021,000	$ 8.10	36.5
1978	4,229,000	3,354,000	$ 8.66	36.8
1979	4,463,000	3,565,000	$ 9.27	37.0
1980	4,346,000	3,421,000	$ 9.92	37.0
1981	4,188,000	3,261,000	$10.82	36.9
1982	3,905,000	2,998,000	$11.62	36.7
1983	3,948,000	3,033,000	$11.94	37.1
1984	4,383,000	3,406,000	$12.13	37.8
1985	4,673,000	3,659,000	$12.31	37.7
1986	4,904,000	3,848,000	$12.47	37.4

Source: U.S. Department of Labor, Bureau of Labor Statistics.

EXHIBIT 8 Construction Industry Worker Employment by Type of Construction, 1977–1986 (000 omitted)

Type	1977	1978	1979	1980	1981	1982	1983	1984	1985	1986
General building contractors										
Residential	443	485	473	408	368	318	352	416	452	473
Operative	54	54	54	40	33	24	30	31	31	30
Nonresidential	369	416	462	452	424	395	369	415	452	455
Heavy construction contractors										
Highway and street	208	225	239	227	204	178	192	204	215	228
All other heavy construction	408	469	532	518	515	480	434	436	437	419
Special trade contractors										
Plumbing and heating	355	397	413	400	388	361	364	417	447	463
Painting and decorating	104	116	124	119	109	101	108	126	133	136
Electrical	262	287	314	320	320	309	306	342	375	406
Masonry and plastering	263	292	313	303	279	256	276	325	355	395
Carpentering and flooring	95	104	102	92	88	76	91	108	117	134
Roofing and sheet metal	107	126	133	134	125	121	130	148	155	167

Source: U.S. Department of Labor, Bureau of Labor Statistics.

Appendix   National Labor Relations Act as Amended by
*H.R. 281**

* * * *

Sec. 2. When used in this Act—

* * * *

(23) The term "employer" includes any person acting as an agent of an employer, directly or indirectly, but shall not include the United States or any wholly owned Government corporation, or Reserve Bank, or any State or political subdivision thereof, or any person subject to the Railway Labor Act, as amended from time to time, or any labor organization (other than when acting as an employer), or anyone acting in the capacity of officer or agent of such labor organization. *Any two or more business entities engaged primarily in the building and construction industry, performing work within the geographical area covered by a collective bargaining agreement to which any of the entities is a party, performing the type of work described in such agreement, and having, directly or indirectly—*

   (1) substantial common ownership;
   (2) substantial common management; or
   (3) substantial common control;

   shall be deemed a single employer: Provided, That the existence of a contractor-subcontractor relationship between any two or more business entities working at a construction site shall not, by itself, be deemed to create a single employer or be considered as evidence of direct or indirect common management or control, within the meaning of this sentence.

* * * *

Unfair Labor Practices

* * * *

Sec. 8(d) For the purposes of this section, to bargain collectively is the performance of the mutual obligation of the employer and the representative of the employees to meet at reasonable times and confer in good faith with respect to wages, hours, and other terms and conditions of employment, or the negotiation of an agreement, or any question arising thereunder, and the execution of a written contract incorporating any agreement reached if requested by either party, but such obligation does not compel either party to agree to a proposal or require the making of a concession: Provided, That where there is in effect a collective bargaining contract covering employees in an industry affecting commerce, the duty to bargain collectively shall also mean that no party to such contract shall terminate or modify such contract, unless the party desiring such termination or modification—

---

*Changes in existing law made by the bill, as reported, are shown as follows: existing law proposed to be omitted is enclosed in black brackets, new matter is printed in italic, existing law in which no change is proposed shown normal text.

(1) serves a written notice upon the other party to the contract of the proposed termination or modification 60 days prior to the expiration date thereof, or in the event such contract contains no expiration date, 60 days prior to the time it is proposed to make such termination or modification;

(2) offers to meet and confer with the other party for the purpose of negotiating a new contract or a contract containing the proposed modifications;

(3) notifies the Federal Mediation and Conciliation Service within 30 days after such notice of the existence of a dispute, and simultaneously therewith notifies any State or Territorial agency established to mediate and conciliate disputes within the State or Territory where the dispute occurred, provided no agreement has been reached by that time; and

(4) continues in full force and effect, without resorting to strike or lock-out, all the terms and conditions of the existing contract for a period of 60 days after such notice is given or until the expiration date of such contract, whichever occurs later:

The duties imposed upon employers, employees, and labor organizations by paragraphs (2), (3), and (4) shall become inapplicable upon an intervening certification of the Board, under which the labor organization or individual, which is a party to the contract, has been superseded as or ceased to be the representative of the employees subject to the provisions of section 9(a), and the duties so imposed shall not be construed as requiring either party to discuss or agree to any modification of the terms and conditions contained in a contract for a fixed period if such modification is to become effective before such terms and conditions can be reopened under the provisions of the contract. Any employee who engages in a strike within any notice period specified in this subsection or who engages in any strike within the appropriate period specified in subsection (g) of this section, shall lose his status as an employee of the employer engaged in the particular labor dispute, for the purposes of sections 8, 9, and 10 of this Act, as amended, but such loss of status for such employee shall terminate if and when he is reemployed by such employer. Whenever the collective bargaining involves employees of a health care institution, the provisions of this section 8(d) shall be modified as follows:

(A) The notice of section 8(d)(1) shall be 90 days; the notice of section 8(d)(3) shall be 60 days; and the contract period of section 8(d)(4) shall be 90 days.

(B) Where the bargaining is for an initial agreement following certification or recognition, at least 30 days' notice of the existence of a dispute shall be given by the labor organization to the agencies set forth in section 8(d)(3).

(C) After notice is given to the Federal Mediation and Conciliation Service under either clause (A) or (B) of this sentence, the Service shall promptly communicate with the parties and use its best efforts, by mediation and conciliation, to bring them to agreement. The parties shall participate fully and promptly in such meetings as may be undertaken by the Service for the purpose of aiding in a settlement of the dispute.

Whenever the collective bargaining involves employees of a business entity comprising part of a single employer in the building and construction industry, as defined in section 2(2) of this Act, the duty to bargain collectively, for the purposes of this section, shall include the duty to apply the terms of a collective bargaining agreement between such business entity and a labor organization to all other business entities comprising the single employer and performing the work described in the collective bargaining agreement within the geographical area covered by the agreement.

* * * *

(f)[It] shall not be an unfair labor practice under subsections (a) and (b) of this section for an employer engaged primarily in the building and construction industry to make an agreement covering employees engaged (or who, upon their employment, will be engaged) in the building and construction industry with a labor organization of which building and construction employees are members (not established, maintained, or assisted by an action defined in section 8(a) of this Act as an unfair labor practice) because (1) the majority status of such labor organizations has not been established under the provisions of section 9 of this Act prior to the making of such agreement, or (2) such agreement requires as a condition of employment, membership in such labor organization after the seventh day following the beginning of such employment or the effective date of the agreement, whichever is later, or (3) such agreement requires the employer to notify such labor organization of opportunities for employment with such employer, or gives such labor organization an opportunity to refer qualified applicants for such employment, or (4) such agreement specifies minimum training or experience qualifications for employment or provides for priority in opportunities for employment based upon length of service with such employer, in the industry or in the particular geographical area [:]. *An agreement lawfully made pursuant to this subsection shall impose the same obligations under this Act as an agreement made with a majority representative pursuant to section 9(a): Provided,* That nothing in this subsection shall set aside the final proviso to section 8(a)(3) of this Act: *Provided further,* That any agreement which would be invalid, but for clause (1) of this subsection, shall not be a bar to a petition filed pursuant to section 9(c) or (e): *Provided further, That any agreement lawfully made pursuant to this subsection may be repudiated only after the Board certifies the results of an election conducted pursuant to section 9(c), in which a majority of employees in an appropriate bargaining unit either selects a bargaining representative other than the labor organization with which such agreement was made or chooses not to be represented by a labor organization.*